What They're Saying about Dudley Shearburn and Emily Wilson:

"I have been laughing my head off at Dudley Dovel Shearburn for 50 years. And between howls of laughter, I've marveled at her good sense and big heart. Now she's summed herself up and recorded her wit and wisdom for all of us for all time. Hooray!"

> *ANN WALDRON,* author of biographies of Caroline
> Gordon, Hodding Carter, and Eudora Welty.

"Emily Wilson is to oral history what Scheherazade was to story telling. She doesn't stop until she gets the whole story. She is intrepid, indefatigable, and irresistible."

> *MARGARET SUPPLEE SMITH,* co-author with Emily
> Wilson, *North Carolina Women Making History*

Since the publication of *Get A Good Life* in October 1996, the book has gone through four printings and sold 1,000 copies to friends at home and readers as far away as Amsterdam and Tallapoosa County, Alabama. We have gone on the road to entertain audiences from Critz, Virginia, to Longmont, Colorado, and we have made new friends and kept the old. Our stories of how Dudley lives her life and how that life became a book have connected with people across the generations, as well as across miles. But our bookkeeping has been somewhat erratic as any readers might guess.

So in the spring of 1999, two weeks before Mother's Day, we were joined by two new enterprising women, Cheryl Schirillo and Susan Tague, who agreed to market the book. Thus, a new edition for a larger audience and an opportunity to up-date the life of Dudley Shearburn as told to her friend Emily Wilson

Get A Good Life ended with Dudley's contentment in a small apartment in downtown Winston-Salem. That chapter has a new ending: Last year Dudley moved into a 900 sq. foot upscale art-deco loft space. But there's more to that story: the biggest fire in Winston-Salem history threatened but did not destroy beautiful Albert Hall, and today Dudley is once more entertaining friends as they exclaim about the city skyline from her fourth-floor balcony.

Dudley has led new book groups--"Great Love Stories" and "Pulitzer Prize Winners"--and she has led new travel groups--to Greece, France--and to the new Guggenheim in Bilbao, Spain. And she has a new grandchild--Joseph Charles Shearburn--her seventh. The good life goes on.

With this special Mother's Day edition of our first book, presented at the Whistling Women in downtown Winston-Salem, we pass a milestone in publishing history: we still have not had a cross word. So it's on to the next book about Dudley's travels, beginning with her move from Gray Court Apartments on Broad Street in Winston-Salem to 101 North Chestnut Street in Albert Hall, near the City Jail, God's Acre, the Post Office, and a good coffee shop.

Dudley says, "The best thing about this book is that Emily and I have made so many new friends. That's how you make the good life even better."

Dudley and Emily

Get a ^good^ Life

by Dudley Shearburn
as told to Emily Wilson

To Roxy with my best regards,

Dudley D. Shearburn

Library of Congress Catalog Number: 99-61663

ISBN: 0-9670974-0-1

Additional copies may be ordered using the form
at the end of this book through:

WildWood Press
2616 Village Trail
Winston-Salem, NC 27106
(888)922-5254

Limited edition Printed by
Sir Speedy, Winston-Salem, North Carolina

First edition 1999
Printed in the United States of America

For my seven precious children

Brice Will Pick Mary (to) Fitz Martha('s) John

Contents

About the Authors

Dudley as Described by Emily

My friend Dudley Shearburn is a trip. I mean she's a serious traveler: during the twelve months we were trying to write this book, she went to Europe three times and spent five weeks in San Francisco and two weeks in St. Louis. Dudley also travels in her head. Just this week she is teaching herself French feminism, French feminism! That's equivalent to teaching yourself to be a brain surgeon. And the beauty of Dudley's trips is that she takes her friends with her, one way or the other.

Dudley is a born teacher. I've learned how to tell a silk purse from a sow's ear just by trailing her through junk stores I would not have gone in on a dare if she hadn't been there to take me. She helped me find a silk purse for $5 in a Birmingham thrift shop, and I can tell you that purse has gone to some of the best places. The best! I act as if I ordered it from Neiman-Marcus, and not from the sale catalogue either. I also have a grapevine basket Dudley gave me for my birthday ($6 from W.R.T. Consignment Shop). A very sophisticated woman from New York City

1

(who finds the South somewhat quaint) picked it up and looked at it and would have bought it off me that minute had I not said. "That's an original grapevine basket by Dudley Shearburn, please do be careful." She put it down, carefully, and afterwards she walked about my house with a good deal more interest. I have one little bowl, which I use for peanuts when somebody like a Nobel Prize poet is coming to dinner—just a plain white ceramic bowl of a kind my mama had in the kitchen. I like the feel of it in my hands, and its plain look. I like it because I saw it at Dudley's apartment when she was serving peanuts for one of her parties, and when I admired it, she said, "It's yours, sugar. Take it home." I say it's on loan, but she says it's mine. Dudley is the most generous friend in the world.

Also, Dudley is a kick. I mean a kick! She has both feet on the ground most of the time, but she's also perfectly capable of levitating. When Dudley starts her stories (which we all know by heart now), she lifts us up and out of our everyday lives and carries us into hemispheres where laughter is the music of the goddesses. Dudley can make you laugh so hard you cry and cry so hard you laugh. And I've seen her do it with young and old, bohemians and high society, liberals and conservatives. (Dudley is equally at home entertaining friends in her weekend trailer at Highway 21 Mobile Home Park and at the local Mary Symington Book Club meeting

Wednesday afternoons.)

Dudley makes us feel good. I can't, for the life of me, understand how she works this magic, except she loves people, all kinds. She really, truly does.

If you have a problem you can call her up and ask her to meet you at the Rainbow Cafe and pour out your heart; and she'll listen and reassure you and give you a few helpful hints—about how to teach, or parent, or get over a divorce. If you want to find the perfect present for someone but don't want to spend more than $10 max, you can ask Dudley to take you to one of her favorite shops and she'll show you how to find it. If you want to make a change (big or small), but are afraid to take the first step (travel alone, have a party, wear something a little more outrageous than you are known for), Dudley will even lend you a short skirt. Always, she'll steady you with her look of delight and say, "You can do it! And you will be just perfect, perfect."

Dudley thinks nothing of leaving home at 4:00 a.m. to drive five hundred miles to see family and friends (Dudley's driving is matched only on the NASCAR track). She manages to go to Europe twice and sometimes three times a year when she doesn't have any more money to spend than some people spend on their pets or their lawns (she has neither). She knows how to fix up, make over, make do, spot a treasure, make a place for it, and enjoy. Her treasures are silk purses, and a few sows' ears made to look like silk purses. Me, I'm a silk purse. Dudley tells me so all the time. And I believe her, because Dudley is my friend. When you read her stories and listen to her advice, she'll be your friend, too.

Emily As Described by Dudley

Why do I love Emily? She tells the truth. Emily doesn't fool around. She cuts right to the chase, and states unequivocally how it is. And that means I can't be flip about what I say (well, sometimes I can). And that means I have to think about what I say and it makes for good conversation.

Emily's straight forwardness can be disconcerting. She has a sharp wit and a tart tongue. Unexpectedly, my friend can come out with the most outrageous statements. Her descriptive comments about people often make me roll with laughter. She's usually right on target. She can sniff out phoniness in 30 seconds, she debates an issue with devastating truth, and she will spar with anybody. The powerful don't bully Em.

But Emily is a poet, and she thinks with a poet's logic—in grand and grandiloquent terms. Her creativity is boundless. She hatches up some miraculous plans—like buying a dear and beautiful cottage in Swansboro by the sea, a retreat place just for her. Then she invites me down.

She'll swear she doesn't cook well, but dinner at the Wilsons' is unequalled for warmth, hospitality, and good food. Sharing food is as natural to her as breathing. I'm included in the Christmas Eve dinner celebration every year. One year I was in San Francisco for Christmas, I sent Emily three Christmas presents. I wanted to be sure I kept my name on the Christmas Eve dinner list.

Emily was born and brought up in Columbus, Georgia, not more than thirty miles from where my grandmother Holley's people are from in Alabama. I tell her all the time I'm sure we're kin to each other, somewhere down the line. We care about the same things. Both of us are tender and vulnerable about our precious children. (We both drive our adult children crazy, sometimes still treating them like babies.) We're probably lost sisters, soul mates, or kissing-kin. In all the years we've known each other since we met as teachers at Salem College, we've never had a falling out.

Emily Wilson is the most tenderhearted person I know. She fights for the underdog, gives her energy to good causes, stands up for her principles, jumps to rescue a friend, and takes me to lunch when I'm broke. As my grandmother used to say, she'll stick by you through thick and thin. She does, she has, she will. Now do you see why I love Emily?

Introduction
by Emily Wilson

Can a woman with little money and big dreams get a good life? Certainly, as long she's willing to look at every day as an adventure. A good cup of coffee, a good book, a good friend, a good bargain, as well as a good walk in Paris—each one excites and delights Dudley Shearburn. Dudley was born knowing how to have a good time, and more than a half-century of experiences has only whetted her appetite for more: seven children and seven grandchildren, classes and reading groups, Fabulous Parties and High Teas, thrift shops and travels, and stories. Dudley's friends believe they've lived her life just from hearing her stories. You'll find resemblances to your own life and discover that yours has more possibilities than you ever imagined.

Get A Good Life is the book Dudley's friends have begged her to write (and the book all her children were afraid she might write—but relax, kids: Mom does not tell all). If you want to down-size and upgrade the way you live, *Get A Good Life* may be the best gift you give yourself this year. Read it aloud, pass it around, and write or call Dudley in Winston-Salem, North Carolina (336-721-1957) and sign up for one of her book groups (Dirty Books and Clean Living?) or one of her trips to Paris (picnicked in a cemetery lately?), Greece (the overnight ferry is a trip in itself, even if you are on the wrong one), England (make friends at the B&Bs), or San Francisco (four days on the train with an eight-year-old, passing through a snow storm).

For weeks this past winter as she was stuck at home in Winston-Salem, Dudley made good coffee, tossed her blonde hair back, and laughed and talked as I sat at the computer and wrote it all down. Dudley's other friends in St. Louis, Dadeville, Chicago, Lagadas, Paris, and Fletcher Park Road, Wyoming, were so envious that we had to promise to send them copies of the conversations. So, here are some of Dudley's tips about how to live, re-live, or invent a good life. It's not money that counts. It's family and friends—and doing things, going places, telling stories. From her childhood in Alabama to her life as a single mom in St. Louis to her class-rooms in North Carolina to her walks in Chichester, England, Dudley Shearburn lives the good life.

One quick question before you meet Dudley: have you booked your reservations for a millennium party? Dudley has hers—in an elegant hotel in Galway, Ireland. All her children and her grandchildren are invited. Her friends are furious—they will not be left out of the next adventure. So, don't tell Dudley, but let's all meet her and the other Shearburns at the Great Southern Hotel in Galway on December 31, 1999. Dudley loves surprises. Meanwhile, get started on fixing up your life by reading about how Dudley fixed up hers.

Chapter One

Get A Philosophy
Martha Stewart's Not the Only Act in Town

When I was growing up in Birmingham, Alabama in the 1940s, we shared what we had and we talked a lot—people talked all afternoon and all evening. I just kind of knew that having friends around took the edge off some of the harsher parts of life. We had rituals for entertaining. We always expected someone would drop by on Sundays or we got on the streetcar and went to Grandpa Dovel's on a Sunday afternoon or we sat on the porch reading the Sunday paper and invited somebody to stop in when they walked by. One of my grandmother's sisters would come over with her husband: Aunt Irene and Uncle Joe had a car, and they'd come by on Sundays and we'd take rides. Being with other people somehow seemed better than being by yourself. When I was in high school, my family never got upset if I invited 12 girls for a spend-the-night. Everybody brought her own bacon and eggs for breakfast the next morning. Sometimes there were so many people I'd sleep in the bathtub just to get away from them. There's not any way to live except with other people.

When you're growing up, you're a listener by and large; and you're happy to be a listener because you're finding out interesting stuff. You pick up a lot they don't talk about outside the family circle. So you have access to some stories you might not otherwise hear if you didn't have people coming around all the time. Isn't that where Southern writers like Eudora Welty and Lee Smith got their stories—listening to what was being said? I think everybody has a good story, even in bad times. I know we did.

In Alabama it's often hot, so you have to sit still, and that's what we did with our afternoons. It was too hot to do anything else. We sat in the rocking chairs on the back porch or around the kitchen table early in the morning, too hot to move. Or we sat on the porch. We read the paper, talked to each other, and hoped someone would come visiting so we would have someone to talk to. Happiness was company coming to our house. For my grandmother it meant people cared and paid attention. She was pleased to see friends come up the sidewalk as if they were giving her a present, had done her a favor. People were very important to her; and then to me.

What you learned from company and kin-folk and friends and neighbors and whoever came by was what life is all about; and even if you didn't understand, it came back to you later, and you'd say, "Oh, that's how marriages go," or "Oh, that's why they were unhappy about some-body's not going to school." You learned the

11

things that your family really cared about—how delighted and impressed and pleased they would be about a second cousin, blood kin, graduating from high school. Your connections mattered. So you realized that your family was going to be equally happy when you did something that was an accomplishment. All those people weaving in and out gave you a background or a cluster or some kind of string of people before and behind you that cared.

I could tell when they were talking about something that they disliked or were heartbroken or concerned about. My grandmother and her sisters dropped their voices. Their faces would change. The whole temper of the front porch would change. I knew when it was something they disapproved of—a husband who drank—or something which broke their hearts—a cousin who committed suicide. I remember they'd say, "It's terrible that happened, but we'll get through it." A kind of acceptance, that's part of family, too. We talk about it, we know it's there, we go on, and we will go on, and it's okay. We'll make it, we'll get through, and we'll do it with spirit, with joy. We'll pick out the good stuff.

And that's my philosophy of life.

Chapter Two

❧

Get A Family
A Tale of Two Grandmothers

In my Alabama childhood, Grandma Sis—on Daddy's side of the family—used to say all women should sleep in silk nightgowns, own good jewelry, and wear cashmere and a fur coat. Grandmother Ada Ballard Holley—on Mama's side—used to say, "Use it up, wear it out, patch it up, or do without." When my sister and I went to spend the weekend in the big brick house on North 30th Street in Birmingham, where Grandfather Dovel (Daddy's daddy) had been chief designer and engineer for Sloss-Sheffield Steel & Iron Company, his chauffeur came to pick us up in a custom-built Cadillac limousine with fringed shades and vases of fresh flowers at the windows. My sister, Alice Marie, older by fifteen months, and I waited in our three-room apartment in West End, an old blue-collar neighborhood near the coal yard and railroad tracks. Grandmother Ada's husband, Moses Calvin, used to walk the tracks to pick up coal for our stove (my mother was divorced, working for $15 a week and we were living with her parents).

Our next-door neighbors, the Bozemans, kept a cow, which they pastured in a city lot. The

13

cow was important because they could sell buttermilk for five cents a pitcher. During the depths of the Depression, the Bozemans and my grandparents tried to find work and to stay warm and kept a pot of black-eyed peas on the back of the stove.

Over at Grandpa Dovel's, my sister and I slept in Grandma Sis's silk nightgowns, went to the beauty shop to have our nails painted and our hair done (set in a Marcel wave), and for every Sunday dinner we had Lady Baltimore cake and ice cream for dessert. Grandpa had a refrigerator (there was an icebox in our apartment), a telephone (number 32496), and a library. Among the leather upholstered furniture, there were glass bookcases with a set of the History of the Great War (WWI), World Book Encyclopedia, and the Book of Knowledge. In summers, when they took up the oriental rugs, my cousins and I would lie on the hardwood floor and read—I looked up "Alabama" and "blast furnaces" in the encyclopedia. One year my daddy (James St. Real Dovel) gave us a big world atlas for Christmas. I was fascinated and I read that atlas (I learned to read when I was four). I was born wanting to travel.

Back in our apartment, Alice Marie and I and Mother (Mary Nelle Holley Dovel) all slept in the same bed, kept our clothes in one chifferobe, and mostly lived in the kitchen. My grandparents had a room to themselves, and my mother's younger brother slept on a cot. When there was a fire going in the stove, we'd sit around and read—the newspaper, the Bible, and the Saturday Evening Post. When our utilities were turned off because we could not pay our bills and the collectors came, Grandmother told us to hide under the bed. Alice Marie and I giggled, which upset my grandmother because the collector was walking around outside trying to find someone at home.

And so all of this (and a whole lot more which came later) gave me my philosophy of life: "We're not poor," I said to my grandmother. "We have a lot of fun." My family laughed, and we have been laughing ever since.

Tips for making the most of your childhood

Choose your family well, or use well what got handed to you.

Learn how to tell the difference between a silk purse and a sow's ear and when to use each.

Learn to make do on a little and make out on a lot.

Chapter Three

✦

Get Smart
The Art of Making-Do

If you weren't born in Alabama and you didn't have Grandmother Ada to tell you, you might need to know that a sow's ear is a pig's ear. It meant something only fit for a pigpen—rough and inappropriate for certain company. Grandmother Ada would talk about "sleazy" material—of the sow's ear variety—and she taught me to prefer Egyptian and Sea Island cotton to mill ends. I was probably six or seven when I went with her to buy material at Loveman's department store in downtown Birmingham—or Levy's dry-goods store in the neighborhood. We'd spend a lot of time—my grandmother would walk around and around those counters, feeling and naming material. Mr. Levy— short, bald-headed—would say, "Miz Holley, what do you think about this?" She made shirts for my granddaddy, and she made our school clothes. I have a quilt, which she made with scraps from some of my dresses. Now, my granddaughter Holley loves to go over the quilt and have me tell her about those dresses. My sister and I had princess-style dresses with piping down the front seams with an inset sash that tied in the back and hand-made button-holes for the placket. If you didn't make it right, she'd say it'd look like a pig's eye. (Grandmother Ada grew up on a farm and raised pigs, which I guess accounts for her vocabulary.)

When I was about nine, Woodward Park in our neighborhood was having a fashion show, and I was going to compete. I got some money from my mother—probably a dollar—and I went to the dime store and bought some red and white checked cotton and some bias tape to make a sleeveless summer dress, without any help from my grandmother. When I brought it back, my grandmother was furious because I didn't have a pattern, I didn't know how much material I needed, I had not bought enough to make anything. She said it was going to be "skimpy." But for better or for worse I had to use it because I had spent a dollar, and she cut a pattern out of newspaper for a little four-gored skirt. She worked and worked on that thing to get something cut out of that little piece of material. I basted on the bias tape, and she stitched it on her treadle sewing machine. I wore it to the fashion show, and it didn't win a prize, and I knew it wasn't going to win a prize. Walking up to that park, I knew my dress, just like Grandmother said, was skimpy.

My grandmother did handwork, and when all the high school girls were wearing crew neck sweaters with round-collar dickies my grandmother made by hand organdy Peter Pan collars with Valenciennes lace. She worked for the money for material—her sisters paid her to help with their children and clean their houses, and she took in sewing. She had learned "quality" because she'd been determined that her one beautiful daughter—my mother Mary Nelle—would be the best dressed child in Powderly, Alabama. Growing up, my mother had pink taffeta sashes and eyelet embroidered skirts. My grandmother would show us my mother's childhood pictures and talk about the dresses.

By the time I was in high school, I had a really good background in how clothing should be made, how sewing should be done with French seams and blind-stitched hems, hand-stitched collars. I knew all that stuff. I knew those were the characteristics of good clothes.

I knew the right fabric for the right thing: good wool for a pleated skirt so that the pleat would stay in. A good natural fabric wouldn't wrinkle much. You could tell the feel of the fabric on your skin. You could tell how it would drape. I really learned about the various weights and qualities of different materials. I learned thread-count; the more threads in a square inch the finer the thread and the finer the material. The smaller the thread count the more sizing (or starch) they put in the material to make it look better—but when you wash it, the sizing leaves, and you have an inferior piece of cloth. All that kind of information.

My grandmother was never happy with the way I sewed. I sewed too fast and didn't finish. I would say I sewed for the "effect"; and she said, "One day that 'effect' is going to fall off of you because you don't sew it very well." I was a senior in high school, and I had made this flowered dimity cotton dress to go to a watermelon-cutting party in my boyfriend's backyard in West End. I had made the dress in a hurry, of course. I had put the zipper on the wrong side and upside down, and my grand-mother was correcting me. Just as I was walking out the door, she grabbed that material and said, "One of the gores of this skirt is wrong-side out." And in my flip way, I said, "Don't worry about it. It's in the back and nobody will see it. And as you always say, Grandmother, it will never be seen on a galloping horse. Nobody's going to notice it."

I wore that dress for two or three years, but once my grandmother had pointed out the flaws, I didn't love it anymore.

The summer before I went to Birmingham-Southern College, I made all my clothes—and I knew they had to be right. I really wanted to fit in and look nice, and I did what my grandmother told me to do that whole summer. Pinking and steam-pressing the seams, basting in the zipper—I spent my summer doing that. I made a maroon satin long-waisted dress with a flared skirt. I probably paid $1.50 a yard and that was good material. I wore it with my mother's maroon suede shoes for my first tea dance, and when I danced the skirt swirled and showed the satin-backed crepe on the underside. I knew it was exactly right. We jitterbugged, and Jimmy Ogle ogled my legs and said, "That is a good dress for dancing."

Over the years you develop a sense of what's elegant, what's quality and what's not, what's good for you. Anyone would love a pretty dress with a satin yoke and rhinestone buttons with a Patullo-Jo Copeland label. But how to find it and afford it?

One day I was poking around in a Veteran's Village second-hand store on Waughtown Street in Winston-Salem, North Carolina, where I now live, and I saw this fabric on the floor. I picked it up. It was one dollar. I realized it was this great designer dress—it still had the label from the best store in town—Montaldo's. But the dress had moth holes on the edge of the frayed hem, and I just looked at it and knew all I had to do was take the hem up a half-inch. And it was a wonderful dress. I first wore it to a big party I gave in St. Louis at Christmas when I invited all my old friends. It was the first year my ex-husband was married to his new wife, and they were going to be at the party (I had invited them). It was a knockout dress, it really was. I felt good in it. You know when you have on something top-notch; it makes you feel good. You feel good and others know you feel good. You've pulled it off. Nobody has to tell you.

And you know when you look like a floozie. Recently I walked into a tea in the library at Salem College, where I teach, and the older alums were there. I knew my skirt was too short and my heels were too high. The first thing I saw were skirts just below the knee and Sunday pumps with a trim heel and one good piece of jewelry on the jacket lapel. And there I was in a black skirt five inches above the knee with a purple silk jacket and a pink and turquoise blouse, and I said, "Uh oh. This is a Rainbow Cafe outfit." I should have known better on a Sunday afternoon at the Salem Library. So I stood in the back of the room because my skirt was so short I didn't want to sit down. (There are ways to correct your mistakes.)

Tips for knowing the difference between a silk purse and a sow's ear

Shop just to learn, in really good stores, to see what is high quality.

Read good fashion magazines and pay attention—I read W, I read Vogue, I read Bazaar, I read Mirabella. You can get most of them in the library.

Pay attention to what people wear when they are photographed at big events. Do they look good? Is it put together just right?

Look around you and decide what people in the community dress well and ask yourself "How can I achieve my effect?"

You learn good quality and good style by trying stuff and having it not work.

Think about where you're going as well as what you're wearing.

Sometimes it is better to dress down than to dress up. The simple black skirt and jacket and good jewelry really do work.

Just because something has a spot on it doesn't mean it's not beautiful to buy at a bargain price. Sometimes you can hide the spot.

Listen to sales clerks to pick up tips, but don't let anybody make you feel bad about your own tastes.

You are your own best judge of a silk purse and a sow's ear.

Chapter Four

Get Married, Get Divorced & Get the Children

Bringing Up Mom

In Alabama in 1949 I was twenty years old, a junior in college. In my family you were getting to be an old maid if you weren't married by twenty-one. Then I met Everett Brice Shearburn, Jr., from El Dorado, Kansas, at Jimmy Ogle's house (Shearb was a traveling man and worked with Jimmy's daddy). I'd never seen anybody like him in Alabama, and that's the truth. Here was a handsome, sun-tanned, dark-haired man, who wore white bucks, gray flannels, and seersucker jackets. They didn't make men like that in Birmingham. He was five years older and had been a lieutenant in the Navy; he had a touch of gray at the temples. I fell in love, of course. The weekends he was in town, we dated, and we married when I finished college. By the standards of those times, he was a perfect choice: he had a good job and good prospects, he was good-looking, he had a great sense of humor, and he was fun at parties. He was everything girls were supposed to look for.

There were a few differences between us, as my grandmother pointed out to my Aunt Love on the porch swing one day. He was Irish Catholic, a Republican, and a Yankee, but she allowed he was "a right nice boy." I don't think Shearb was ever totally comfortable with my big Southern Protestant FDR-Democratic family, especially when we were all talking and laughing. Anyway, we married and moved to St. Louis and had seven children in eleven years. And I thought it was simply the most wonderful thing I had ever done in my whole life. I was happy every time I was pregnant. I'd never seen anything more beautiful than those seven little children.

As a method of survival, I learned some short cuts to child rearing. My first rule was, never say "no" unless a child was going to hurt himself or herself physically, or do something immoral, like bashing another kid over the head. That worked then, works now that they are all grown.

I wanted my children to be creative. I suppose I believed in permissive parenting. When my first-born, Brice, was two, I discovered I could keep him quiet by putting him in an empty tub with a jar of finger paint. Those colorful swirls delighted and entertained Brice, for a while. All I had to do was shower him and the tub at the same time, and I wasn't too particular about either—just a quick rinse, really. He was such a placid baby, patient, too. I wasn't paying a bit of attention to the fact that Shearb came along to shower and found himself standing in finger paints. "What difference does it make?" I'd ask.

Mothers used to use playpens, and I discovered that a year-old baby was a lot happier in a playpen if I gave that baby a brand-new box of soda crackers. By my reckoning it took about an hour and a half for a really determined baby to unwrap the box, take out the packets of soda crackers, open the wax paper, and carefully smash every cracker. It was worth the cost of the box of crackers for another hour's sleep in the morning. And of course, the crumbs did not bother me.

My children all loved to play in the mud. I guess all children like to play in the mud. One of their favorite picnics was to go to a lovely little park overlooking the Mississippi River. One day I'd promised them a picnic, but that afternoon we got a driving rainstorm. We went to the park anyhow. And they found sliding down the sliding board and skidding across the mud puddle at the bottom was more fun than a sun-shiny-day picnic. Afterwards, I piled them all back in the VW bus, drove home, and they were happy, muddy children. It was one of our best picnics. I herded them through the basement door, filled the washing machine with warm soapy water, took the agitator out, and stood them up, one by one, in the washing machine. We soaped off the dirt. When I finished bathing those little children, I wrapped them in towels and set them up on the dryer, put the agitator back in the washer, and threw in the muddy clothes. It was a routine I repeated often—after sandpile play, digging holes in the backyard, and playing in forts.

Keeping children clean seems to be the major part of motherhood. And I struggled. I found it an almost insoluble problem: if they ate supper before they took their evening bath, they came to the table gritty and grimy, a somewhat unappetizing sight. Five little boys and two little girls can be pretty dirty. I tried bathing them before supper only to find that at the end of the meal the smallest children had soup and jelly all over their clean pajamas. One day I got a bright idea. I put three dirty little boys—Pick, John, and Willie— in the tub before supper, put in some squirts of dish soap, suds-upped the water, and brought in a platter of food. I sat down beside the tub with a platter of cut-up wieners, Franco-American spaghetti, applesauce, and bread and butter. Actually it was kind of relaxing sitting there cross-legged saying, "Here's a bite for you, a bite for you, and a bite for you." What a grand idea! I bathed them and fed them, three at a time.

I probably need to say there were some repercussions. One morning at breakfast, Shearb appeared at the kitchen door for his cup of coffee. He didn't eat breakfast with us; it was too traumatic. He seemed a little nervous. He paused for a moment, and then drew a deep breath and said, "I'm not sure I can take this." I think his hand was shaking a little bit. He said, "I'm the only man in St. Louis who has to shower with spaghetti in the bathtub drain."

You develop a lot of short cuts, and—how do I want to say this? People divorce for a lot of reasons, and I guess spaghetti in the bathtub makes for a slippery marriage.

But I had those seven precious little children, and I never forgot who was the most important. I looked for more short cuts. I found out that in the summer if after their baths I put them in their Buster Brown knit shirts and pants, all they had to do in the morning was get up and go outside and play. Like Robert Louis Stevenson's poem, in winter it was quite the other way. I dressed them in their snuggly Dr. Denton's at night, and they were dressed for play in the house the next day. When we went on hikes or picnics or adventures in the woodlands, I dressed every Shearburn, one and all, in red banlon knit shirts. They were more easily identified when I needed to round them up.

If you give seven birthday parties a year, year after year, you get to be an authority. I chauffeured small groups of children to practically every museum in St. Louis. (Maybe that's why my son William is a St. Louis art dealer now.) Tuesday night was the free night at the St. Louis Art Museum, and as the children grew older supper in the restaurant and a walk through the mummy room became a fairly regular event.

Birthday parties outside the house were

better than parties inside the house, so I'd tax my brain for adventurous trips with a Volkswagen bus full of kids, my seven and their friends. We cooked breakfast in Tower Grove Park, we went to the brewery, we went to Grant's Farm to see the Clydesdale horses, we visited the St. Louis Arch at the riverfront, we walked through the old court house and learned about the Dred Scott case. We went to the Eugene Field Toy Museum, the Jefferson Historical Museum (for the Lewis & Clark exhibit), took picnics to the Bellefontaine cemetery (we liked looking at old tombstones, a good way to learn history). I don't think the Shearburn children ever felt like somebody had a better birthday than they did. They liked inviting their friends, and we always came back to the house for a home-baked cake decorated just for the birthday child. We always made a big to-do about birthdays because when there are so many children in a family you need to take every opportunity you can to single out one child for special attention. I made cakes in the shape of fire engines with peppermint stick ladders on the side. I made rocket ships like the one the space walkers landed on the moon—baked in a round mixing bowl to look like a moon. I made tiered cakes with ruffle skirts and a doll in the middle for Mary and Martha. When the children were little, I always let them choose the kind of cake they wanted and stayed up the night before the birthday stirring it up. I didn't use cake mixes—

some children wanted chocolate, some wanted marble, I love coconut (Martha complains to this day she didn't like coconut for her birthday, but when you get to the seventh child, I guess you don't pay attention sometimes).

And so I had those seven babies and had a good time doing it. By the time the oldest was fifteen and the youngest was four, I'd decided that their daddy and I weren't as comfortable living together as I was living with the children. So I packed up Brice, Pick, Fitz, Mary, John, Willie, and Martha; and on a sunny day in October 1967, I found us another place to live. I had decided that I could get a good life for me and the children, and with a lot of love and luck and many hard times, it turned out just that way. (It also turned out that Shearb, too, made a good life for himself, and now when we all get together, he laughs at all my funny stories, even the one about spaghetti in the bathtub.)

Tips for Rearing Children

Falling in love may not necessarily be the only reason to marry. Ask your grandmother for advice.

If you do marry, discuss having children before the honeymoon is over.

If you are going to have two children or more, decide who is going to bathe and feed them.

If you have seven children (or more), devise a shortcut to remember all their names. In our family, Mary and her third grade friend Janice Unger made up a sentence for the Shearburns: Brice Will Pick Mary (to) Fitz Martha ('s) John. (Translated: Brice will pick Mary to fix Martha's John.) I use it often now that I am somewhat older and a little forgetful.

If you can afford it, a separate children's bathroom is a good idea.

Decide what's most important to you about the family and build your life around that.

Don't leave home unless you take the children with you.

Chapter Five

Get On with it
More About Children

Just going to the shoe store to buy shoes for seven children is nerve-wracking. I bought shoes at a place in St. Louis called Lipshitz Shoes. Mr. Lipshitz had been in the shoe business fifty years, and all the other businesses had left, and he was still down in this old, old neighborhood. And I would go in there with those seven children and buy them two pairs each—a pair of school shoes and a pair of dress shoes. Mr. Lipshitz was a little man, and he had to go up ladders to get the shoes. The children never wanted what you wanted them to have. Fitz would never wear anything but black high-top tennis shoes. Sunday, play, whatever, he wanted black high-top tennis shoes. He would be standing there with his great big eyes and saying, "Mama, I don't like those. Mama, I don't like those. I want some black tennis shoes." John, on the other hand, would only wear Hush-puppies, which cost more than others. He would lie on the floor and scream. In the meantime, Mr. Lipshitz would be running up and down those ladders. I felt so sorry for him, trying to please those children. Mary couldn't have anything but brown brogans with a fringed flap because that's what the nuns said she had to wear to school. She would sob because she couldn't have patent leather. Brice could wear only a certain kind of Buster Brown because he had to wear a corrective shoe, and by the time he was thirteen he was sick and tired of them and furious. So buying shoes was a terrible thing to have to do. We'd go on Saturday when I had the car and of course it was the busiest day of the week. We shopped with Mr. Lipshitz for years and years and years, and he was as dear and kind as he could be. The children still laugh about those trips to buy shoes.

I used to take all seven of those children shopping because there was nobody to keep them. Who was going to keep seven children? I'd go down to Famous-Barr to buy clothes and I'd take all the children. And you know how escalators are—you put one kid on, then two, and by the time I got to the top I couldn't find a single kid—they'd be gone in all directions. One day we were going to Famous, and as we started to get on the escalator, I said, "Okay, the three older ones are going to take care of the three younger ones. Brice, you take Mary. Pickering, you take John. Fitz, you take Willie. And you're responsible: hold their hands. Each one of you hold on and wait." So we got up to the top, and I started counting heads—"one, two, three, four, five, six"—and then I said, "Oh, my God, I told you to take care of each other. Where is the baby? There are only six kids here." And Brice said, "Mama, you're holding the baby." And sure enough, Martha was right there in my arms.

So I then decided to shop when some of them were in school. One day I was shopping and I had the little kids, five instead of seven. It didn't seem like so many. I was shopping and watching the kids out of the corner of my eye, and all of a sudden, I couldn't find Fitzmaurice. I started looking around and finally I found him in an alcove behind a row of clothes, which were hanging up. And I said, "Come on, Fitz, let's go." When I got us to the parking lot and Fitz started to get in the car, he pulled his little hand out of his pocket, and he had a stack of price tags about two inches high. He had been systematically removing them from the garments on the rack while I shopped with Mary, John, Willie, and Martha. I decided, "Oh, the store manager will figure it out."

I often ended up taking most of the children to the grocery store. Some neighbors of ours had given Willie an old pipe and he was entranced with that pipe. One day I was in line in the grocery store and the children were running around, and William called to me from the aisle. He had his pipe in his mouth and he said, "Can I get some of this cherry tobacco?" Those people turned around and looked at this seven-year-old with his pipe. I just said, "No, not today, honey."

We used to laugh in my neighborhood

that I went to the A&P so often that I took my phone calls there. I'd be shopping and the manager would say, "Dudley, the phone's for you." My friends knew if I wasn't at home I probably was at the A&P buying groceries. And oftentimes I met my friends there.

Taking the children to the pediatrician was another challenge. I suppose all mothers become attached to their pediatrician because it's such a fearful time, and if they're at all kind to you, you feel like they're the most wonderful people in the world. After my first child was born, on the recommendation of my woman ob-gyn, I started going to Dr. C. Read Boles. He was a young bachelor, just starting out. Really easygoing. He was just the most comforting person in the world. And when that first baby would cry with the colic, I'd call him and he'd say, "Rock him, walk him, love him." And I'd say, "Dr. Boles, it's the middle of the night." And he'd say, "Uh huh, rock him, walk him, love him." Some years later, by the time I had four children, Dr. Boles had married and had his second child. I went in one day and he looked like death warmed over, so haggard. And I said, "What's the matter?" He said, "This second baby stays up all night." And I said, "Rock him, walk him, love him!"

We'd make appointments for check-ups, and he'd take out those seven file folders and line them up and start going down the list. I'd sit out in the waiting room with the little ones and watch the fish in the aquarium while he saw the older ones. When he got to the little ones I'd go in with them, and the big ones would come out and watch the fish in the aquarium. Until one day he said, "You know, this is really hard. I think we need for you to come in for their check-ups on a Sunday afternoon, and I'll see all the Shearburn children then." And that's what we did.

Then of course there were all the different things the children did that I had to take them to. When you have seven children and you multiply their "learning experiences," it is an astonishing number. From the time they were old enough to be involved in lessons, they had t-ball, softball, ice-hockey, football, tennis, swimming, karate, horticulture at the botanical gardens, violin, piano, Scouts. They took art lessons, French lessons, Spanish lessons, sewing lessons. They went to the history museum and to the art museum. Did they rebel? Sometimes. Fitz did not like to take piano lessons, and one day he was determined I was not going to make him go. He was about eight, and he'd been taking about a year from Mrs. Johnson, the old neighborhood piano teacher. I was dragging him out of the house one day, and he had his red and white John Thompson music book in his hand, and I was pulling him down the steps, and he dropped his music book and this paper fluttered out. We had an old typewriter on the third floor, and Fitz used to spend a lot of time up there trying to learn how to type. I picked up this paper, and it was a letter he had typed on the typewriter, and he didn't know how to make the paper stay in, so it was all crooked, wavy. It said, "Dear Mrs. Johnson. I hate piano lessons. I hate you. Your house smells. Your wig is crooked. You have bad breath. And you fart too much. Fitz." It was all true. And I said, "Fitz, honey, you go right out in the backyard and play. You don't ever have to take any more piano lessons." As an afterthought I said, "Fitzmaurice, what were you going to do with that letter?" And he said, "I was going to give it to Mrs. Johnson, that's what I was going to do with it!" So Fitzmaurice switched to a five-string banjo, and he loved it and to this day he plays the banjo.

By the time I got to the last children, I really didn't think it was so urgent that they learn to play an instrument.

More Tips for Rearing Children

Hang loose.

Do the things that give you the most joy. (I loved to sew and knit, which gave the children clothes at the same time I enjoyed doing it.)

Know when to hold them and know when to fold them. You just give up when you fold. I folded a lot. I gave up. It's too much to fight with children. You fight when it's a hard, fastheld principle that you really believe in. Driving and drinking beer—you just know that is one thing you have to stop. But give up on what makes you look good—like children who can play musical instruments—and find out what the child likes to do.

Chapter Six

Get Real
All I Have Left to Say About Children

Martha, my 17-year-old, was standing in the kitchen trying to iron a shirt for herself, and she had put this cotton blouse on the ironing board not having sprinkled it. It was bone dry, wrinkled from the dryer. She picked up the iron and started trying to get the wrinkles out. I said, "Good grief, you can't iron a heavy cotton shirt without sprinkling it!" And then I looked at Mary laughing and standing at the sink, and I said, "And look at you. You can't sew, you can't hem-stitch, you can't knit, you can't cook." And Martha and Mary looked at each other and rolled their eyes. Then Mary snapped her fingers and did a little dance step, and Martha fell in line. "Yeah, Mama," Mary said, "but we can dance!" And then we all laughed and hugged.

Final Tip for Rearing Children

If you can't teach your children to iron, let them teach you to dance.

Chapter Seven

Get A Home
Upscaling & Downsizing

I've lived in big houses, and I've lived in medium-size houses, and I've lived in little houses. From the time I was in high school, we lived in a big two-story house with a kind of shaky back porch and in need of paint. My mother paid $4,000 for it in 1943. I loved it. One of the things I loved was everybody had a sitting room; everybody had a place. My mother had a big bedroom with a fireplace on the second floor. I had the two small back rooms, one for a bedroom, one for a little reading room. (My sister Alice Marie married in '44 and no longer lived at home.) My grandparents mostly stayed downstairs, where they used the back porch to sit, the front porch to swing, and the living room for nice company. (Aunt Love and Uncle Jess, who didn't have any children, kept a spic and span house.)

As a child I had learned something about two-story houses. If people dropped by, as long as the downstairs was straight, it was okay. We didn't pay much attention to the upstairs. (My grandmother's idea of washing windows was to turn the hose on them while she was outside watering flowers.) So, when I got married and started having babies one after the other— my first child was born nine months and 18 days after I got married, and they came almost every two years until there were seven—I thought if a two-story house was good, then a three-story house would be heaven. When Shearb and I had been married eight years and had four children, we bought a great big turn-of-the century upscale house on a private Street in St. Louis with sixteen rooms and a full basement with seven rooms. My mother was appalled. The first time she came to visit she said, "Good Lord, Dudley, you could lose one of the children in this place." My mother was very funny. I said, "You got the idea." And sometimes I did lose them, but they came down when they got hungry.

Of course the thing I hadn't thought about a big house is you had to clean it. I had married a man who'd been a lieutenant in the Navy (the Navy must be the cleanest place in the world), but I found it difficult to tend to all the details. My husband, the man who now is my friend in St. Louis, really did come home from the office one day, pick up the telephone, and say to me, "You forgot to dust under the receiver." He'd point out that the dust on top of the refrigerator was getting deep. At 5'2", I could not see the dust on the top, so it didn't bother me. When he walked in sugar on the kitchen floor, he said, "This place is filthy!" And oatmeal in the baby's hair gave him the heebie-jeebies.

I was in desperate circumstances. I began to develop more short cuts. These are invaluable tips for people who have to clean house.

That house on Hawthorn Boulevard (about 7,000 square feet on three floors) seemed to me to have miles of wall-to-wall carpeting. As my husband pointed out when we first saw it, the whole downstairs was carpeted in carved Wilton. "100% wool," he noted. "It will last forever." (When I left Shearb, it was still looking lovely.) What I noticed about the damn carved Wilton carpet was that supposedly it needed vacuuming every week.

I developed a system because I wanted my husband to be happy. I vacuumed once a month, quick, in the middle of the room. And the other three weeks, on Friday, I got out all the vacuum paraphernalia: the Electrolux tank, the suction tube, the four or five different pieces to clean upholstery, drapes, crevices, baseboards; and I scattered it all around the living room, leaving the vacuum in the middle. I did that every Friday; and when Shearb came home after 5 o'clock, I said, "I am utterly exhausted. I vacuumed the whole downstairs with the children running in and out." Sometimes I'd tip the picture frames to show that I had been dusting everywhere. It worked. He didn't know the difference.

This led to another, even better discovery. We had this mammoth kitchen and butler's pantry built for maids, for sure. We didn't have any maids, of course. My ex-husband was a mid-Westerner and an only child. His mother kept a spotless house. He didn't understand the Southern notion that my aunts held to: when you had one baby, you had help one day a week; when you had two babies, you had help two days a week; when you had three babies, well, whatever. I had seven children, and I sure didn't have a maid seven days a week. I was the maid, like most wives are, or were, or are expected to be. That was part of the marriage package, still is. So back to this kitchen. The floor was black and white marbleized Armstrong linoleum. It had to be scrubbed and waxed. So I stumbled upon this solution for the kitchen: After I had scrubbed it and waxed it and let the wax dry completely, I carefully covered it with newspapers. One time I had cleaned the floor on Tuesday. Shearb was out of town, and I had spread the newspapers carefully. The thing is I had been so hurried that by Friday I hadn't taken the paper up. It was beginning to get shredded and shaggy, but when Shearb came in from his business trip on Friday, he said, "Oh, I see you just mopped the kitchen." And in my head, I said, "What a great idea! I'll just put newspapers down every Friday and tell him how tired I am from mopping." It worked. I bet I didn't mop that kitchen but once every couple of months, though we did have a lot of shredded paper around the house.

When I was expecting Willie, the sixth, I realized I needed some help. Jeannie LaRose came into our lives. She was seventeen and needed a home, and I arranged with Catholic Charities of St. Louis for her to live with us, go to high school, and help with the Shearburn children. Jeannie was the most energetic, cheerful person you could possibly wish for, and she stayed with us five years. She tended to kids, packed lunches, walked kindergartners to school, and helped me clean on Saturdays. She got to finish her education, she traveled with us, and she had a family and a neighborhood of friends. To this day Jeannie laughs about the bottles and the diapers. (She's married to a wonderful husband, with a beautiful house, and an excellent job, but no children. She told me she'd changed enough diapers.)

Of course there was another thing about housekeeping you had to decide to ignore: the other houses on the block. I learned that back in San Antonio, where we had lived five years earlier. I had two children and was expecting a third. Even then, I was stunned by the time it took to keep things organized. We had a six-room ranch house, and my neighbor across the street, Myrtis Burney, was wonderful. She was the paragon of the 1950s housewife. Her six-room ranch house was always perfect. Her husband was a captain in the Army. One day Myrtis said, "Dudley, your laundry has been hanging on

44

the line for three days." To tell you the truth, I hadn't even missed those diapers. Not wanting to appear a sloven, on the spot I made up a big lie. I said, "Myrtis, I just read a research article that says moonlight and evening dew have disinfectant properties. And I want my babies' diapers to be really sanitary." And serious Myrtis Burney believed every word of it. In fact, she told some of the other neighbors about it as a good household hint. And I never told her any different.

Tips for Keeping Your Head While All About You Others Are Keeping House

Don't get caught up in chasing dirt. Dirt won't hurt.

Cheat. Use any method you can, just so it looks okay on the surface.

Don't rearrange the furniture too often because if you do you'll have to wash the woodwork behind it.

Never, ever move a refrigerator, unless you are ready to move from the house. What's under it may frighten you to death.

Don't try to be the best on the block. Competition is for the Olympics.

When I left Shearb, the seven children and I moved into a three-story townhouse in the mid-city of St. Louis, two blocks from St. Louis University. It was called "a new town in town" and was a HUD project. It was named LaClede Town, a small enclave, a self-sufficient kind of village, carefully planned for the Great Society of the 60s. This was the pristine example of urban housing, the hot spot in St. Louis. Dick Gregory lived in LaClede Town, and St. Louis baseball players—Bob Gibson, Lou Brock; visiting musicians dropped by the town tavern—Jeanie Trevor, the Allman Brothers. It was cool, and I was there. I was newly divorced, a certified teacher with my first full-time job, and making steps toward graduate school. LaClede Town was a good place for us because it was vibrant. There was a lot of action. There was a cross-section of people, and everything children needed was within the confines of "the town."

The house was attached to another just like it, three stories, but small. Very small. But I could still live out the notion—boys on third floor, girls on second, and a place to entertain on first. There was a bathroom for the boys, one for the girls. Then I began to notice the boys kept coming down to use the girls' second floor bathroom. We had been used to a lot of space in a big house. Now in this narrow three-story townhouse, space was limited. Pickering had established his art studio in the third floor shower with his oil paints spread out, his easel in the corner of the shower, his canvases in the linen closet, and his charcoal sketches taped to the wall. Scaling down wasn't as easy as I'd thought it would be. With three boys in one room and two boys in the other, it felt as if there would not be an inch for anybody else, but there was. And here's how it happened.

I was accustomed for many years to going down to the Soulard Market early Saturday morning at 5:30 and buying enough food for the week. Every week one of my purchases was seven gallons of milk, a gallon a day. Milk took up two-thirds of the refrigerator. I began to notice that the seven gallons weren't lasting all week, which seemed strange. Sitting at the table one night, I realized the three oldest boys had a guest. He was a big ole' boy, big black beard, curly hair, broad shoulders. He drank down one glass of milk in a gulp, poured himself another glass and said, "Boy, I love milk." And I said, "Do you, Dan? And Dan, where do you live?" And he said, "Mrs. Shearburn, I live here. I've been living on the third floor with Brice and Pick for three weeks." That's what happens when you never go to the third floor. Dan was a school dropout. He stayed about six months, and Dan Bridges was a truly kind and serious person. He was a great asset to our family. He had not been tended to much in his growing-up years, and he enjoyed being in a family. He was a star pupil in an alternative high school for dropouts; and when he finished his high school credits, he earned a full four-year scholarship to Earlham College, paid for by the Danforth Foundation.

The night when I realized that Dan had been living with us and I hadn't known it, I learned that a small house can be stuffed with people, crowded to the rafters, with a supper table hardly meant to seat four that now seated nine, and that a small house has a lot of warmth and joy. It offered a great sense of family. When Dan got that scholarship, he turned it down to join a commune in Arkansas, and he said, "Dudley, I never had much of a family. I think family life is wonderful. And I chose this commune over that scholarship, because that's what I need." We heard from him for many years, and he was happy. When he came to St. Louis, he brought us bread, which the commune made and sold.

The LaClede Town house was a tiny, tiny house, in terms of what we'd been used to. Having a place for myself was hard to find. I solved the problem by putting ropes across the living room doorway to keep everybody out but me and company when they came. Actually, the ropes were gorgeous—gold drapery tiebacks— and the first time a kid came from next door, he said, "What's this? A museum?" I had brought the ropes from the Hawthorn house, from the good draperies, and they made the statement: this

is my place, kids. Did it work? Part of the time.
Unless the teenagers had company and they
wanted a place. Then I'd have to go to my tinier
sitting room upstairs, which was also a bedroom,
office, reading room. No, I wasn't miserable.
Why not? Because reading was the great escape.
I've always said my degree in English saved my
life. I just removed myself. As long as I had a
chair, a lamp, and a stack of books, it was my
place.

Tips on Using Your Space

Get rid of what you don't need, which is what you have to do when you downsize (I got rid of clothes I had needed to throw away for a long time and big pieces of furniture, like a dining room suite).

Keep the meaningful, quality pieces that you treasure because of their relationship to some thing in your life (the original oil paintings in the big house found a home in the little house).

Learn the meaning of double-duty (a bed is a sofa, the kitchen table will serve for any kind of dining, the washing machine makes a functional beer cooler when you have a big party).

Find out what kind of space is right for you. Great big can be cold and lonely. Small can be warm and cozy.

Living two blocks from St. Louis University made it easier for me to go to graduate school. The children's activities in that little village were all within walking distance, and they had things to do while I was in school. It worked. It was the right place at the right time. Later, LaClede Town, sad to say, was a failure in terms of housing in the Great Society. It wasn't well kept up because government funds were cut, and in that place in the city, it began to attract people in economic distress, people dealing in drugs, people from broken families. The friends we had there have all gone on to better educations, better jobs, better incomes. But LaClede Town served us well. I finished my degree, and in 1977, I moved to Winston-Salem, North Carolina. I was Dr. Dudley Shearburn, associate professor of education at Salem College. I was forty-seven years old, with one child still living at home, and we moved to 314 Banner Avenue in Washington Park. It was a small 1929 cottage in an old neighborhood, with small rooms and a big yard, close to the college. Very cheap and in need of repair. The price was $27,000, and I borrowed the money from Pfefferkorn Mortgage Company and began to pay it off. In a few years, I refinanced to add a family room, a deck, and a whole bath, re-do the kitchen, screen in the back porch.

When Martha graduated from Salem Academy (she got tuition remission because I taught at Salem College), we had a big Shearburn party. Children came from all their places—John from Vanderbilt and Willie, home from two years at Lake Forest College; Brice from California (he was in law school and working full-time); Pickering, home from the Marines, at Quantico officer's training, and his wife and new baby; Fitzmaurice, getting ready to start summer school at Washington University, but already in business for himself; and Mary, living in Winston-Salem and training to be a nurse.

We all managed to find a place to sleep by using sofas and pallets. It was Old Home Week, all crowded together in one place again. The house on Banner Avenue had one advantage—it had a beautiful back yard, and we had the party there. It was the end of May, the shade trees were wonderful, and we strung a hammock between two trees for the first grandbaby (Pickering and Geneva's little boy, Cullen St. Real). We put a pony of beer on the back porch, we grilled hamburgers and wieners on a Weber grill, and Martha and her Salem Academy friends got all dressed up in their pretty dresses and partied till the sun went down. The seven Shearburns were some happy children, and I was a happy mother. "The baby," dear Martha, had finished high school.

But I was glad they were not all going to be staying forever. Once again, I was having trouble keeping my own space. When they weren't there, I used a very small room that just had room for a twin bed and a chest, but by then I had come to love small, cozy rooms. When they all came home, I was glad I had a single bed so nobody had to sleep with me, and the room was too little for anybody but me.

Tips for Family Living

If you buy a small house, be sure it has a big kitchen and a big yard.

Insist on two bathrooms, even in a little house.

Count the closets. There were three. We built three more.

Keep some square footage for yourself, even if it's only 8' x 9'. A door that closes is a "must" for your room.

In 1991 when Mary was the mother of a four-year-old (Holley Dovel), I said one day, almost on the spur of the moment, "I think I'm old enough to have a place of my own." Mary and Holley could stay at 314 Banner Avenue; it was just right for mother and daughter, across from the park. But I was moving. I truly, truly wanted to live by myself, for the first time in my life. I was sixty-two, January 8.

In March I got a tip from a friend about an apartment available in this great, right-down-town 1929 building—I loved downtown. I was a city girl. I loved the bright lights and the sirens, but more than that, I loved the grace of this old apartment building. 10-foot ceilings, hardwood floors, arched doorways, and best of all, mauve and black Art Deco tile in the bathroom. It was just about 700 square feet. And it was mine, all mine, for $275 a month, including heat and hot water and private parking. I moved in.

I feel like I'm in a luxury apartment. Not only do I have a bedroom of ample proportions, but I have the loveliest little sitting room I also use as an office. I also have my favorite reading chair which nobody sits in but me, with a hassock just right for my short legs, and a red taffeta pillow for my back (from Pier One, for $5), and a knit throw to keep my toes warm (a gift from my daughter Mary). And right within arm's reach, a stack of books and a stack of magazines, my great extravagance, periodicals delivered to my house—I can't seem to give them up. There's something utterly satisfying about this urban apartment. My sophisticated friends walk in and say, "This looks like Manhattan." And indeed, it does. It's a 14 x 18 living room that does extremely well for drop-by company, Sunday brunches, or wine and cheese parties for thirty people. This apartment is exactly right for me. It's mine.

I have the best of all possible worlds. My granddaughter Holley lives with her mother, but because her mother works the night shift as a nurse, I get to keep Holley some evenings. (Her Uncle Brice baby-sits her other times.) I share my space with Holley, but I have taught her that when I am busy she entertains herself. And she does, in the small sitting room with her crayons and pencils, while I'm sitting in my favorite reading chair. Holley loves the quiet and the independence and the solitude that she has there. She also keeps two drawers full of dress-up clothes, for when I'm busy (I am busy; I prepare for classes and keep appointments with students). There's no television, and Holley has learned to amuse herself and to stay focused on things she's doing, and to enjoy her own creativity. She has a place, and I have a place.

Tips for Living Alone

Choose the right space, not the right address.

Get to know the neighborhood by walking.

Be sure you have off-street parking for a downtown apartment.

Meet the people who live around you.

Enjoy what's in a downtown neighborhood—library, bookstores, bright lights and action, and the sounds of people.

Learn to enjoy living alone, but also keep family and friends around you.

Discover the ambience of place, the charm and grace of an old apartment.

Accentuate the best of what you have (charm,grace) and be content with what you lack (central air, a dishwasher).

Settle in and invite friends over.

Chapter Eight

✣

Get A Bargain
Treasures, Trash, & Trinkets

My fifth child, John, and his wife, Annette, had a second baby girl, Claire, born December 6, 1995, in Amsterdam. They really wanted a girl because they already had a three-year-old, named Emily Dovel (we like family names), and they thought two little girls would be perfect. (My mother and daddy thought two little girls were perfect.) Well, the phone rang in the middle of the night. John was as happy as he could be. He said, "Pud-brain"—a term of endearment— "you have another beautiful granddaughter, and her name is Claire Timmons Shearburn. Annette is wonderful, and Claire is a big girl—9 pounds, 5 ounces." They were taking her home that same day, before she was 24 hours old. (I stayed eight days with my seventh baby. My woman doctor said I needed a vacation.) As happy as I was, I was almost in tears (as I am right now) because I think grand-babies should be born close to their grandmothers, and I knew I would not see that grandbaby until March, when I went to Amsterdam after my women's trip to Paris. I was thinking about her every day and looking at old baby silver to see what piece to send her—from cups and spoons for pabulum given to my children as they were born one by one. I decided on a spoon and a cup, which was given for Brice (he groused a little about my giving away his baby cup, but he had two and I figured he could share), and I would take them when I went.

I thought about Claire's present again when I found a little dress at the Carolina Thrift Store. When I go to a thrift store, I do what I always do: I have certain things I look for. I go to various "departments" and the first department I went to that day was little girls' dresses. Carolina Thrift is a story in itself. I once received a phone call: someone was canvassing the neighborhood, and asked me to put give-away items in a plastic bag and leave the bag on my porch. The Viet Nam veterans would pick it up. I told the lady I didn't have a porch, but if I gathered up some things (my closet needed cleaning out) what should I do? She said, "Here's my number, my name is Linda. Call me back if you decide to put out some stuff." I hung up the phone. And then I thought, good gracious, she must be calling for an organization that has a thrift store I don't know anything about. I immediately called her back and asked her where the things were going, and she gave me directions to Carolina Thrift in Greensboro, run by the Viet Nam veterans. Addicted as I am to junk stores, within the hour I jumped into the car (it was raining and there were predictions of bad weather, but I went anyway) and drove straight to the store in Greensboro.

Carolina Thrift is housed in a large old supermarket, which went out of business, with checkout counters first thing when you walk in. To get the most out of a thrift store, the first thing you have to do is realize that somewhere in all that junk there are some treasures, and you can't be put off by disarray and dirt. So, I started on my usual pattern: first, little girls' clothes. I've been buying dresses for Holley at thrift stores since the day she was born. (I bought a red dress with white smocking from Alabama Thrift in Birmingham and a beautiful $1.98 sailor dress— the best— from the Goodwill Store, also in Birmingham. When they get in the $4 range, I don't buy them.)

So, back to the Carolina Thrift on the day I found Claire's dress. There are long aisles with racks and racks of second-hand clothing. At the beginning of each row there is a lopsided hand-printed sign that tells you categories of clothing. I spotted "Girls under 5 years" and as I was looking through the rack, I began to feel sleeves and shoulders. I discarded nylons and polyesters and fabrics I call "sleazy." Nylons and polyesters feel silky, but clearly they're not silk—you tell the difference by practice. There's something about a natural fabric (silk, cotton, wool, linen) that is more giving, more relaxed, and yet sturdier. People buy nylons and polyesters because they are cheaper, and sometimes they stand up to wear longer, but not necessarily better. I don't like them because they are not gentle and hospitable to the skin, especially children's. There was an announcement over the loudspeaker: "Thank you, customers, for shopping today at Carolina Thrift. We hope you're having a good day and want to let you know that all items marked with a yellow tag are 50% off; with an orange tag, 75%; and the red tags today are regular price." So now while I'm feeling the materials, I'm also looking at the color of the tags. (There were at least one or two customers in every aisle, and a wonderful conversation was going on among three men. They were arguing about when Bob Hope and Frances Langford visited the troops in World War II and what band Langford sang with. I couldn't remember, but one of those guys said, "I was there and I know she sang with Jimmy Dorsey.") You get a lot when you go to a thrift store, besides the shopping. Watch the people. In the next aisle, there was a man with two women trying to decide on an outfit for one of the women to wear to a funeral. She did not want to buy what he was holding up—an odd black jacket and an odd black skirt (odd means they don't match). She said she didn't have to wear all black. The other woman, who must have been the mother in the family, was losing her patience. She said, "Just take this, it's only for a wake, you don't have to wear it after that" and she was agreeing with the young man. I moved on down the aisle, and they were still trying to decide.

When I found the perfect dress for Claire, I saw the smocking, and then I saw the lace. I recognized the lace as a good, fine, tiny, cotton lace that used to be used on little girls' clothes. I know from trying to find some recently, it's hard to find—you have to special-order it. Good lace comes from France. The little round collar was on a rose-pink dress with light, tiny turquoise flowers for a tiny girl. The collar was edged in this gathered lace. I turned the collar up and could tell the lace was hand-gathered and carefully whipped on with little tiny blind stitches (stitches you can't see from the front), which told me the dress was hand-made. Already I could see a photograph of Claire in that dress, and her mama would know this was one of her best dresses. Luckily, it had a yellow tag—half-off. The original price was $3.98. I bought it for $1.96, plus NC sales tax, total $2.08.

At home I hand-washed the dress, dried it on the shelf over the radiator, and as soon as it was lightly damp I got out the ironing board, the spray starch, and happily and lovingly ironed it. Perfect puffed sleeves. No spots, not a one. Cotton does not seem to me to take any longer to iron, and ironing is one of the things I love to do because when you get through everything looks so perky. I learned to iron from watching Grandmother Ada, and by the time I was in high school

I ironed my own clothes. The secrets to good ironing are be careful about the temperature (cotton is not so easily scorched) and use starch (I was telling Holley, who was with me when she came home from school, that when I was growing up we had to make our starch, light or heavy). Life is easier now; you have a can and you spray lightly. It took about 20 minutes, while I talked to Holley. When it was finished I hung it on a hanger on the door knob and couldn't bear to put it in the closet for a couple of days because I got so much pleasure out of realizing what a beautiful gift that was going to be for Claire Timmons Shearburn. Then we sat down— Holley to read and write, and I to read and write, preparing for my class in French feminism at Salem College.

Chapter Nine

Get Some Fun
Great Parties, Cheap & Easy

Entertaining is different depending on whether you're trying to make a good impression or trying to have a good time. It was different when I was married and living in middle-class St. Louis, entertaining my husband's business friends and when I was a graduate student or teacher entertaining whomever I wanted to. And I discovered that I preferred the freedom and fun of not feeling under pressure to do things in the so-called "proper" way. Having to find a new circle of friends in graduate school saved me.

The best advice for entertaining is: be yourself. Invite people you like or you see and think you'd like to get to know. You have to really say, "It's my life, and I'm going to have fun," and the way you do that is to extend yourself a bit and see what kind of people you really like. Take some risks every now and then by inviting different kinds of people and don't spend your time in the kitchen fussing with fancy menus. Save the time to talk with your guests.

And don't worry if parties don't always work. Sometimes I ended up having invited the wrong people to a party, and I learned. For example, in St. Louis I was working in Democratic politics, and I invited a lot of campaign people to a party. One of them was a very handsome man with a city political job, and I told him to invite anybody he wanted to. The night of the party, late, three people walked in with the man I knew—three big burly men in double-breasted cashmere overcoats, smoking cigars, and I said, "Who are you? You look like East-side gamblers." And wouldn't you know, that's exactly what they were. In a situation like that, you just make them a part of the group, stand next to your most reliable male friend, and don't invite them again. Interestingly enough, they were as uncomfortable as I was, and when conversation came to a standstill, they left, with their felt hats and double-breasted overcoats. It made a great story, and really, no harm had been done.

I like to invite about a dozen friends after work, and the party is over early, before 9:00 p.m. (It's not my responsibility who leaves with whom, but I do make a point of noticing if anyone has had too much to drink: if so, I ask someone to drive him or her home.) By and large, I invite people like me—interested in education, books, movies, conversations—and I try to have different ages. At my own parties I mix and mingle, I pat and hug. I hope there's always a sense of friendliness and fun, humor, and lightness. The host or hostess creates the atmosphere, and you hope everybody's having a good time.

We send out the message we want to send out. My message is that I'm glad you're here, you're part of the circle, I want you to be part of the circle, but I'm not looking for a mate. I like my life as it is. Some single women clearly are needy and hunting and wanting, and people take advantage of that. At your own party you're saying "no" to anything more all along by the way you present yourself, in the way you keep things light. You let people know that you're happy with the status quo, that's the biggest thing. You have to be pleased with your life and when that's the truth, that's the message. A party is just a really great way to show how much pleasure in life you're finding, on your own, but among friends.

Parties in apartments, like mine, seem better for putting a lot of people in a small space, especially if they are interesting and different. There's something nice about having a party where people stand up and move around and visit and eat pick-up food and feel comfortable about serving themselves. This works well when you have two or three small rooms to congregate in. I think you can put 30 people in my apartment and they'll find little groups to settle into, and conversations gather. I think it's okay to be crowded.

You have a party wherever you are. The place does not limit what you do. What you do when you have friends in has nothing to do with size or place or address or urban or suburban. It has to do with a great collection of people who can move around and find out about each other and strike up conversations and find somebody they never knew before. And sort of marvel at the opportunity.

One of the best parties I've had in my space was entertaining my French friend Alexander. He spent a week with me in Winston-Salem, and I had a lunch, a brunch, and a big cocktail party for him. All my friends came. We ate and drank, we talked, and we made our Parisian visitor feel at home in North Carolina. It was our Southern hospitality. Alex said to me, "This is the way to live, Dudley. Your friends bring the joie de vivre."

Chapter Ten

Get the Spirit
Giving & Receiving Gifts

My mother used to say, "Sometimes it's more blessed to receive than to give." The act of giving is a pleasure to the giver, so if you graciously receive—and you have to learn how to do that—you've warmed somebody else's heart. Don't you think that's true? Or you give somebody something, and the person says, "Oh, you shouldn't have done that."

You learn about receiving and giving gifts from gifts people have given you. When I think about the most exciting, magnificent presents I ever received, the thing I remember that was most wonderful, as a child, was in the middle of the Depression when my mother was having trouble keeping us in school shoes. We'd wear shoes with cardboard on the inside because there were holes in the bottom. We'd wear shoes with strings tied around the toe to hold the sole on, and I can remember my granddaddy sitting in front of the fire gluing a leather sole on a shoe, a sole he had cut out painstakingly to fix my sister's brown oxfords. That being the situation, you can understand how excited my sister and I were when my rich and frivolous Grandma Sis sent us home from a visit to her house with a new pair of shoes. They were the most elegant black patent leather t-strap slippers any little girl could ever have dreamed of. A pair for each of us. We skipped up our front steps to Mama and Grandmother Ada, the happiest children you can imagine, looking at those slippers every step of the way. My mother broke into terrible tears and said, "Have those people lost their minds? These children need school shoes and corduroy overalls and union suits. What can those Dovels be thinking of?"

For all my mother's heartbreak, her sadness didn't affect me very much. I treasured those shoes more than anything I remember. I wore them, I stuffed my feet into them until they rubbed blisters on my heels and toes, and I think that's when I learned that a totally frivolous gift can lift the heart. When I was in high school, I worked in the afternoon and on Saturdays for a flamboyant entrepreneur in Birmingham. Basil P. Autrey was sunny, funny, and drank straight gin out of a bottle from the bottom desk drawer, starting every afternoon about three. My mother had worked for him since I was five years old, and I loved Mr. Autrey dearly. More than once he had been kind to me. This particular time I had been invited to the Old South Ball of the Kappa Alpha fraternity at the University of Alabama, I, a West End High School girl from a blue-collar neighborhood in Birmingham. After school one day Mr. Autrey heard me telling Mother, "Maybe

I shouldn't go." I certainly didn't have the pre-scribed hoop-skirted Southern belle gown. Mr. Autrey pushed his hat back on his head—he always wore his hat in the office—and said to my mother, "Mary Nelle, call long distance and get the number of that big, famous department store in Dallas—Neiman Marcus—and let's get that girl two dresses and have them sent Special Delivery. An Old South Ball shouldn't be passed up by any girl from Alabama."

They were delivered to the office that very week, absolutely, incredibly perfect. The one I wore was mauve gray lace with off the shoulder ruffles, a full, full skirt with two under-skirts, a gray velvet sash with two big cabbage roses at the waist. I'd never felt more beautiful. My KA date—Roy Manly—was my high school sweetheart who had gone off to college. Could anything have been more perfect than to receive at midnight from your dear truelove a silver pin embellished with KA letters, with him smiling and telling you that you were the prettiest girl at the ball?

Sometimes a gift has a history. When I was 30 years old and expecting my fifth precious little Shearburn baby, we moved to the Hawthorn Boulevard house, and I made the acquaintance of the neighbor behind me, Kay Brimmer. Kay is one of those people who is always doing some-thing helpful for other people. Her brother-in-law in New York City owned a company that manufactured women's clothing. A couple of times a year he'd send down a great big box of sample dresses, and scarves, jackets—sort of left-overs. One spring we opened what we came to call one of his CARE packages and out fell this most sophisticated sumptuous silk scarf. It was two yards long, at least 36 inches wide, of a gossamer-silk fabric, and printed in a black and beige tiger print. I wanted that scarf. So did Kay. It was her brother-in-law. She ended up with the scarf. Anytime I went to a party and wanted to look my knockout best, I put on a black dress and borrowed that scarf. The trouble is I wouldn't give it back to her, and usually six months to a year later Kay would say, "Dudley, I want my scarf back," and reluctantly I'd take it to her. One time I borrowed our scarf and casually flung it around my neck and wore it to a cocktail party at Judi and Brian Bender's house. I was leaning up against the wall deep in conversation with probably the only unattached bachelor at the party, when he looked down and said, "Oh, my God, Dudley, you're on fire!" The end of that chiffon scarf had wafted across a lit candle and was in flames. I snatched it off and we stomped out the fire, and I grieved because a good twelve inches of the scarf were ruined. I took it home and cut off the charred end, carefully rolled and finely stitched a new hem, and took it back to Kay, confessing its adventure. She laughed and said, "Never worry," and we both continued to wear the scarf year after year.

I moved to Winston-Salem, North Carolina; Kay kept the scarf in St. Louis. A few years ago I was in St. Louis on my 60th birthday, and my friends got together and had a party for me. There was lots of laughing and lots of reminiscing and lots of story telling. And then I started opening gifts. There was a present from Kay, beautifully wrapped as Kay was wont to do, and I started peeling off the paper. When I opened that box and got a glimpse of those colors in the scarf, tiger-printed black and tan, I didn't know whether to laugh or to cry. The card said, "Dear Dudley, It's a little like us; kind of old and kind of wrinkled, but still a great piece of work."

I have one more story. Sometimes people give you gifts because they have really listened to what you said. After I was divorced and the children were mostly grown, I spent a number of years in a great relationship with a wonderful friend. One time at Christmas he said to me, "Dudley, sugar, tell me anything you want for Christmas, whatever you want. And I'll do my best to get it for you." And I said to my dear, loyal friend, "Don't give me a Christmas present. What I really want from you is time." He was a busy man. I said, "Time is the only thing that really counts." A couple of days before Christmas I came home late from my office at Salem College. I unlocked the door, walked into the living room just as I heard a clock strike the quarter after. In cahoots with my daughter Martha, my friend had brought in a surprise. And there it was, a pecan wood grandfather clock, handmade and softly rubbed—from a clock factory near Mobile, Alabama. There was a big red bow tied around it and another box, wrapped, sitting at the foot of the clock. In the box was a watch with a note, and the note said, "So you will always have my time."

I've been the recipient of the most generous gifts from beloved and warm-hearted people all my life. That's how I learned about giving gifts by having been lucky enough to have received.

It was the good fortune of those givers to have money to buy gifts that were expensive. That's not always the case with me—sometimes I have money to spend on gifts, and sometimes I don't. When I do have money, it's easier. When I don't, I have to think about it more—I have to spend time and thought and creativity to make up for the lack of cash. Probably when I don't have money I try harder to buy exactly the right thing.

Because I often don't have a lot of money to spend on gifts, I'm always on the lookout for gifts that might be suitable for people I care about. It was a pretty exciting day in Birmingham a few years back when I was drifting through one of the second-hand stores and found some elegant percale sheets—soft and wonderful white cotton sheets, top and bottom, with pillow cases to match, the whole set. The problem was they were monogrammed in a deep rose, large stunning monograms, obviously custom done. They weren't my initials, but I did a double take when I realized that the AWW were the initials of my dear friend Ann Wood Waldron. I bought the whole kaboodle for $6.98. I took them home, put them in the washing machine, bleached them out with two packages of kit whitener (it doesn't take the color out of the monograms—it whitens white), dried them, starched them, ironed them, and put them in two big brown envelopes and sent them to Ann in Princeton, New Jersey. Of course, Annie called me and laughed so hard she could hardly talk when I told her where I had gotten them—she's from Birmingham but doesn't buy things in junk stores. She said they were "elegant!" She was going to use them for her best sheets for her guestroom. When I visit, I sleep on them. Once we tried to think of what the name of the person could be, the person who owned those sheets before Annie. We made up some names for the lady who gave them to the junk store: Anita Williams White? Amanda Wilson Whitley? Who slept on those sheets? And why had she given them away? We decided somebody had died and their children had gone through the house and thrown everything away. And let that be a lesson to you and use your best linens now!

The years I lived in LaClede Town near

St. Louis University in the late sixties and early seventies—looking back—seem to have been years when there was neighborliness and care between people who lived near each other. One Saturday morning the children ran in, telling me about our new neighbor. Her name was Lin; her husband's name was Bill. They had a two-year-old girl. The Shearburn children were helping them carry in odds-and-ends of furniture, amusing the two-year-old, and I'm sure had already given the neighbors the up-date on our family situation. I went out on the patio and called across to my new neighbors, welcoming them to LaClede Town. We talked a minute, and Lin Butler, one of the most beautiful people I ever saw—almost 6 feet tall, long brown hair to her waist—looked like moving in was as easy as pie. She laughed and told me it was her birthday. August 1st. She had come from Chicago to St. Louis to work on a graduate degree in counseling. Her husband Bill was in the business school.

It was a Saturday morning and between paydays. I had little or no money and wanted to think of something to give Lin to welcome her. I went back into the house, rummaged round in the kitchen, got a big brown grocery sack and a black magic marker. On the sack I drew a silhouette of the townhouses in LaClede Town and printed in big letters WELCOME. I numbered one of the houses, No. 3, the number of her new house. I opened the cabinet doors and scanned the cans in the cupboard, got out a big, big can of pork and beans, took down a bottle of catsup, and a jar of mustard. I added a can of sliced pineapple, an old can opener, some paper napkins, and then I wrote a note: "This is a busy woman's supper. The can opener is for your husband to open the cans of beans and pineapple. Leave him a note that says, 'Open cans, add catsup, add mustard, put in a baking dish in the oven, and serve with sliced pineapple. And please have it ready when I come home from class.'" I put it all in the sack and tied it up with a long length of white toilet paper, puffing up the bow to look festive, and sent it over by the Shearburn children. Lin Butler and I have remained friends for twenty-eight years.

One of the gifts I loved best which I gave the children took me almost a year to assemble— I got the idea of giving to each child photographs from his or her childhood. The first thing I did was to go through all the family photos. I picked out pictures that made me laugh, looking at those beautiful little children. Two of Brice, two of Pick, two of Fitz, two of Mary, two of John, two of Willie. I could only find one of Martha by herself. (I think by the time I got to the seventh child, I was too busy to take pictures for the baby book.) For Martha's second picture I had to use one of her with Willie and John. All that spring and summer I shopped the junk stores looking for picture frames, 5x7s, 8x10s. I came up with a surprising assortment of quality frames—all wood, some rubbed, one in dark red, one in a forest green, one black and distressed with antique gold. Each time I found one I'd put it in the bottom drawer of my chest, the drawer where I collect future Christmas presents all year long. The frames cost between 99 cents and $2.99, every one with glass. When I started thinking about how to mat and frame them, I decided that the odd-size photographs would look better with some writing to fill up the space in the frame. I spent some time composing words for each picture. I began one sentence for each picture by saying, "There once was a little child named—— — —" and writing the full name. And then I said, "But we called him—or her" and then I wrote in the nicknames. I wrote, for example, "There once was a little boy named Thomas Fitzmaurice Shearburn, and we called him Fitz." Then I wrote a short paragraph for each of the children (I described the child), took the pictures and the paragraphs to a friend of mine, and paid her to copy my words in calligraphy. She helped me arrange the pictures on the mat, cut them to size, and frame each one. It's my favorite gift to have given my grown children—total cost under $100 for seven Christmas presents. When I go visit them, everybody has them displayed and we look at them together.

I've observed the children now that they are grown, and I think they've learned something

about gift giving. Time and thought and something you've made yourself, and tenderness and
love go with the gift. Pickering has been married
to Geneva for 23 years—they married when they
were 19. When I was at their house at Christmas
time, I saw, where it always is, a hand-made
wooden bread bowl in the middle of the dining
table. This is going to make me cry. When the
children were growing up, I had my great-
grandmother's bread bowl. I still have it. And I
often told my children the story my grandmother
told me, that after the Civil War my great-
grandfather walked home from Virginia to Alabama, and soon afterwards he married. For an
anniversary present for his wife after the first
year, he had bought a block of pinewood, shaped
out a bowl, sanded it, and had given it to his wife,
Mary. (My grandmother's brothers and sisters all
named their oldest daughter Mary after the
mother, Mary Ward.) Pickering always loved that
bowl because he loved wood and working in
wood. The bowl that sits on his dining room table
now is one he made for Geneva when they were
19, before they married. He had found a large
square piece of oak and decided it was exactly
the size block he would need to make a bread
bowl for his wife-to-be. He hadn't thought of
how hard it would be to shape oak as opposed to
pine, but for weeks before the wedding he'd sit in
the basement at night with his hammer and
chisel, making a bowl out of that piece of oak. I

used to go down there late at night and find him asleep in the chair in his bathrobe, with his hammer and chisel and the half-finished bowl in his lap. When I was there last, we sat around the dining room table and laughed about how many chisels broke when Pickering was trying to shape out that hard wood. It's clearly one of the most treasured gifts in the house. Why am I crying? Because they still love each other dearly after 23 years of being married.

Tips on Selecting Gifts

Be on the lookout all year for great gifts at good prices and stack them away in a special Christmas-present drawer.

Try to think of the person the gift is for and what that person loves, not what you love.

Mentally consider what you know some-one really wants, and try to fulfill the wish.

Consider one of your own possessions to give to someone else—a piece of costume jewelry a friend admires, a silk scarf that you can pass on.

Shop second-hand stores and consignment shops looking for old pieces, warmed with a patina of age and use.

Be sentimental. Don't be afraid to be a little hokey. A sweetly sentimental gift can touch the heart.

Handmade gifts always carry a special message of love and care.

A small blue ceramic pitcher, purchased in a second-hand store for $4, might be exactly the right touch for a friend with a blue and white kitchen.

T.J. Maxx usually has a good collection of attractive containers at economy prices—$5, $7. Choose one and fill it with a potted dwarf rose bush. Total cost under $15. Makes a nice wedding present.

Think ahead. Six weeks before Easter give a friend a pottery planter from the Goodwill Store, set with gravel and narcissus bulbs, ready to bloom for the holiday. $10 or less.

Try to remember what your friends collect - paper weights, cat figurines, old silver spoons—and poke around the junk stores. Sometimes you can find a piece for the collection for a couple of dollars.

Old guest towels, purchased at a yard sale or a consignment shop, make a nice "bread and butter" gift after being a guest in someone's home. $5.

Everything's A Dollar Store has kitchen utensils for a dollar each. Make up a collection and package it in a brown grocery sack, tied with a colorful new dishrag. It's a good kitchen shower present. $6.

Give a boy-child a shopping bag full of scrap lumber bought at the lumberyard. Add a small hammer and a box of nails. It's a happy gift for under $10.

Buy a little granddaughter a fluffy, tacky nylon nightgown from a second-hand store. Properly laundered, it makes a nifty "play dress-up" outfit. Under $5.

Chapter Eleven

Get An Education
Back to School

In 1968 I was recently divorced and living with seven children three blocks from St. Louis University. The location wasn't totally by accident. When I decided to start a new kind of life and chose LaClede Town, it was because, in the back of my mind, I thought that somewhere along the way I was going to have to go back and get more education. That time seemed a long way off. But I kept meeting people, making friends, and learning about my new neighbors who were in graduate programs at the Jesuit university, St. Louis U. One night at a neighborhood party, I met a college teacher who had come to St. Louis to get a Ph.D. in counseling. He helped me realize that I could do that—I could go back to school.

It wasn't easy. I was thirty-eight years old, and I was scared. I thought everyone on that campus knew more than I did. And that wasn't the worst of it. I dreaded being "old" among those coeds. I was sure I wouldn't wear the right clothes. I hadn't kept up with the Viet Nam War. I had spent my last sixteen years fixing bottles, changing diapers, and hauling kids around. But at the end of August 1968, one hot afternoon, I walked up the hill to the campus of St. Louis University, stumbled around, confused, and found where to register. And got myself started in a master's program in education. I could hardly breathe when I went to my first class: Philosophy of Education. Ninety-two students in a theatre-style room, with a professor who spoke so softly I knew I would have to sit on the front row to hear him. I had to buy nine books.

Taking a class in philosophy was a long way from making hamburgers and chili.

But it all worked out. I met the people sitting around me—we had to work in groups. I began to realize that my tentatively offered opinions were sometimes acceptable. Best of all, I wasn't the oldest person in the class. One evening a neat thing happened: Dr. O'Brien, the instructor, had told us we were going to have a team project. Each group had to present a skit illustrating a great philosopher's thoughts on education. I felt like the way I felt in P.E. class when they chose up sides. I thought nobody would choose me. But an attractive young woman turned to me and said, "Dudley, be on our team. You've got good ideas. We need you, and besides, you've got a lot of moxie."

I'd never heard the word "moxie," and I wasn't sure what it was. But if she thought I had it, and it was going to be worth something, it suited me. I had a lot of fun doing that skit in front of that class and somehow it seemed an introduction to being a graduate student. We did something on Dewey. I wore a real short skirt and dressed like a third-grader. It was funny. People laughed. We got a good round of applause and approval from Dr. O'Brien. We made John Dewey come alive. And I came alive, too.

Ten years later I was teaching at Salem College and advising adult women who had returned to school. It was easy for me to remember just how it felt. Let me tell you about one of my students.

The first thing I noticed about Carol was that every time she said something, she blushed. And she kept feeling the hem of her skirt. I looked over her transcript, not the best I had ever seen, and she began to talk. She said, "I don't think I can do this. I didn't have a very good year in college when I was nineteen. I haven't told anybody in my family that I am going back to school because I'm afraid that I won't do well at it." She looked at me with her blue eyes and her skin flushed, and she said, "That transcript is really bad. I'm in a deep hole, aren't I? I'm afraid I'll never get out of it."

We talked about things like starting out easy, doing things one at a time, picking a subject that really interested her. I asked her what her reasons were for being back in school, how she was going to work it into her schedule, what about her husband, how many children did she have. And I assured her she was going to be successful.

Carol graduated from Salem College with honors in English and won a full scholarship to Wake Forest University for a master's in English. Along with the degrees came a whole new way to look at life. Carol joined a group of women I took on a Paris tour a couple of years ago. We landed in Paris—eight of us—checked into our small hotel on the Left Bank. We hadn't been in our rooms an hour when Carol and I left to walk the streets of the sixth arrondissement, looking for the great church St. Germain-des-Pres. We stopped for coffee at the Deux Magots, Simone de Beauvoir's old haunt. We had our walking map, the sun was shining, it was October, Paris was at its best. Twenty-four hours later my friend Carol went off on an excursion by herself. She was confident she could find the Louvre and walk the Champs Elysses. And of course she did. When we met for drinks the afternoon of the second day in Paris, Carol was laughing and talking and telling us about her solitary adventure. She had ridden the Metro by herself, bought a silk scarf from an Indian street vendor, and was writing postcards back to North Carolina, telling her children what it was like to be in Paris. On her own in Paris.

What I notice about women who return to school is they are all scared, they are afraid they can't do it, they all fear that younger women know more than they do. What they find out is that they are so directed and so focused and so determined that invariably they do well. It doesn't take long. A few good papers, a little good feedback from a professor, a spark of interest in something they've discovered, and they begin to realize, "This is going to be fun." About the end of the first semester, I notice some changes when they drop by my office. They are not wearing skirts and blazers anymore. They are in a good pair of jeans. Not long after that, I see they have a sharp haircut and a backpack for their books.

New ideas, new friends, new challenges, sharing a cup of coffee in the day student lounge, making an A on an exam—those are life changing events. The thing I hear most is, "I love it. I'm doing something for myself. And I get to decide how I'm doing it."

Chapter Twelve

Get A Book
Reading Groups

I'm addicted. There's no other word for it. I'm addicted to words in print. I read the backs of the cereal boxes, the wrappings on the toilet paper. I was thrilled beyond measure when they started printing paper towels with words and pictures. The children have always said that my addiction served them well. When they wanted to ask me something and they were afraid I'd said "No," they always waited until I had my nose in a book. They knew they would have a better chance of my saying "Yes" if I was caught up in the story.

And that's how I got started in reading groups. What I know about reading is that just reading a book is not enough. What you really want to do is to talk about it. So for my very first reading group I thought of Irish literature, something I wanted to read and talk about. Where better to read than in a bookstore? I picked the Rainbow News Cafe, reserved a meeting room on the second floor, put the word out, and pretty soon we had a group of twenty-two: "Ireland by Book and Foot." An additional lure was that people who read the books could choose to go on a trip to Ireland at the end of the reading. There are plenty of folks who claim to be Irish. Gary, for example, came all the way from Greensboro and bought his Irish genealogy chart with him. And you couldn't mistake John when he walked in the first night with two loaves of Irish soda bread. Every other Monday bringing snacks and bottles of wine, we crowded into a dusty, book-lined room. We read Yeats, O'Casey, Joyce, Synge, and the biography of Lady Augusta Gregory. The readers complained about James Joyce (too long, too convoluted, too obscure), but in the end admitted that they felt so touched by his stories they cried. There's always something in a book readers can identify with.

The appeal of the Irish writer is powerful. Six of us went to Ireland and sat on the lakeshore at Coole Park, reading Yeats' poem, "The Wild Swans at Coole." It was a gray, rainy, windy day, and there we were, sitting right in the middle of what Irish writers write about. We could feel their exuberant happiness, always tinged with an undercurrent of sadness and tragedy. We ended up later in a tiny fishing village, Cleggan, where we rode a dirty, oily mail boat across to the island of Inishbofin. The island is mythical, foggy, dotted with gray stones. We walked looking to the west, having the same view the Irish had when they left for America. The Nobel poet Seamus Heaney describes his trip from Cleggan to Inishbofin in a poem: "Sunlight, turfsmoke, seagulls, boatslip, diesel." And we had experienced exactly what Heaney talks about in "Seeing Things." I read the poem often, and it takes me back. What you read is like being there. Just this month I read in the New Yorker another poem about Inishbofin. I said, "I've been there and the poet has been there, and we both know the same thing."

Of course, you can't always go to the places you read about. In a small group of women readers meeting at the YWCA, we read Jane Austen's *Sense and Sensibility*. The early 1800s in England don't seem to be like the 1990s in America, but, would you believe, discussion of the book generated raised voices, table pounding, and wildly dissenting opinions. What could generate that kind of debate, you might ask. It was Austen's emphasis on marriage and on marrying for money. Fran, who had recently moved to the South from New England, said there isn't anything wrong with money. Martha, on the other hand, argued that money isn't the only path to a good life. Each person drew on her own experience, and by the end of the discussion we'd learned a lot about the people in the group. What more could Jane Austen have wished for?

"Dirty Books for the Dog-Days of Summer" is a whole 'nother ball game. We read erotic books, but erotic books highly regarded, not trash. The title of the reading group drew twenty-two women and two men. It takes a lot of savoir faire to teach *Quiet Days in Clichy*, by

Henry Miller. We waded in and talked about it. Women had different ideas from men, and David, who never misses a reading group, had to use a lot of his lawyer's skills to defend the outrageous behavior of Henry Miller, the central character. But in the end, a male-female dialogue did give us all plenty to think about. We probably laughed from embarrassment, having to deal with explicit sexual imagery, but talking about what was in the book gave every reader an appreciation for a gripping plot, elegant language, remarkable descriptions, and characters who struggle.

The other week at the Intimate Book Store I started a new group, not knowing who would come. Fifteen people came: five of them had been in reading groups with me before, but ten I'd never seen. I looked around the room and said, "Look at this, people I've never seen before who must like the things I like and are here to read and talk and make some congenial friends." There's usually a good collection of unattached businesswomen, single or divorced. There are several older women, my age, in their 60s. There are housewives I never saw before but who are there to get some conversation and stimulation and experience something intellectual. They always say, "This is for me. I'm doing this for me."

One of the neat things about a group like that is that very different people come, and one person may hate a book and someone else will say she loved it. And that's what happens in a reading group. Each brings her own personality, her own background.

At the Intimate in another group called "Stories of Love and Lost Love," we've read classic love stories, some about failed love. *Ethan Frome*, *My Antonia*, *The Great Gatsby*, *For Whom the Bell Tolls*, *The End of the Affair*, and *Breathing Lessons*. Most read at least one or two of these books years ago in high school, but as adults they bring a whole different slant to their reading. The greatest fun comes when they find something that seems new; and when someone else mentions the same thing, they feel extra joy in having discovered something together. When people walk out of that reading group, they walk out laughing.

I tell my groups that I read books because, as William Gass says, reading is my knothole I look through to see what's going on out there, the way you look into other people's minds, the way you find out how other people are like you. In every group there is one person (or two or three) who will say, "Oh, I'm like that character. That happened to me. I didn't know it happened to other people." I believe absolutely that reading changes a person's life. Women's lives are in flux, and they are looking for some new experience, some new way to connect, some way to be and to enrich their lives. They discover how characters come through difficult situations, or

91

fail to come through. Women read about other women and recognize the kinds of encumbrances they have, barriers they've had to overcome. The best thing that happens is that women begin to look at characters in stories and say to themselves, "I'm doing okay."

I always like to tell people what I'm reading, and to ask them what they're reading. Right now I'm in the middle of *Age of Innocence*, by Edith Wharton, which I read in the living room early in the morning while Holley is still asleep. In the car, waiting to pick up cleaning or for a class to start, I read *Fried Green Tomatoes at the Whistle Stop Cafe*, by Fannie Flagg. On the top of the stack in the bathroom is a book about Mayan archeological sites (I'm going to the Yucatan in January). In my crowded, book-lined office, I am reading three novels by North Carolina writer Kaye Gibbons for my Salem College course, "Women in Transition." I read *Zorba the Greek*, by Kazantzakis, on a 12-hour flight to Greece. I once missed a flight in Atlanta because I was reading a new Alabama history I'd bought at a thrift shop in Birmingham. While I was waiting in line at the K&W Cafeteria, I cried, reading *The Death of Artemio Cruz*, by Carlos Fuentes.

Reading is the best way I know to get a good take on the human condition without having to leave my living room. When I don't have a trip in the works, I have a book.

Rainy days and Mondays are good times for wrapping up in an old quilt, sitting in the rocking chair in my apartment, and reading to my heart's content.

Chapter Thirteen

Get Away
Born to Travel

I can't remember when I didn't want to travel. From the time I was able to walk around, I was ranging the neighborhood visiting people. In the middle of the Depression, when I was seven or eight, my mother's younger brother, Uncle Billy, left home to hop freight trains. He was seventeen. When he came back one hot summer day, grimy, with a rolled-up shirt under his arm, I thought he was the most glamorous thing I had ever seen. And from that day on, I strongly resented the fact that boys could go where they pleased and it was unseemly for girls to do the same.

Summer mornings invariably found me up with the sun at five o'clock, drifting out the unlocked front door, slamming the screen behind me, and roaming the neighborhood. Early morning travel got in my blood. Even to this day when I leave for a trip, my preferred departure time is three or four in the morning so I can roll along on the highway and watch the sun come up.

The first trip I took I was probably three years old: I ran off down the street to visit some neighbors—they lived almost a block away. My Granddaddy Holley came after me with a crepe myrtle switch, and when he swatted my legs, those little pink flowers flew! It didn't stop me from taking trips.

By the time I was five years old, when I got mad at my grandmother, I'd pack a brown paper sack and walk three blocks to my Aunt Love's house. Aunt Love was not a loving, nurturing person by nature. I remember walking up her front steps one day with my brown paper sack and seeing her sitting in the porch swing with a frown on her face. And somehow I knew intuitively that I had chosen the wrong destination. But that happens to all of us now and then when we take a trip.

I got a wonderful idea about 4:30 a.m. in the middle of a hot summer in Alabama, and it turned out to be a pivotal idea as far as my life was concerned. It happened like this:

My mother had decided to move away from my grandparents in West End. My sister, who was nine, and I, who was eight, lived with her in an apartment in someone's home on the south side of town. There were times when my mother would be out with friends, and she would leave us alone in the apartment. Looking back on that, it might seem odd, but actually the family who owned the house—the Slaughters—lived right downstairs. Well, I woke up with the dawn one morning and realized that my mother hadn't come home that night. I was pretty excited. There was some wonderful sense of freedom about all this. I woke up my sister, Alice Marie, and said, "We're all by ourselves. We need to go to Grand-mother's house." Alice was very reluctant to start on this trip since getting to Grandmother's house involved about a six-mile walk, going through the heart of downtown Birmingham. I was adamant. Somehow in my heart I knew this would be the greatest journey I'd ever take. I said, "We have to pack a lunch," and all we could find in the kitchen was half a coconut cake from the A&P and a warm bottle of 7-Up. But I got my conservative and law-abiding sister hooked into the adventure. Walking down 20th Street in Birmingham with the town just waking up was about the most exciting thing I'd ever done. There was an underpass right downtown. By then it was around 6:30 a.m. I must confess the under-pass was a little daunting. It was dark in there. But I grabbed Alice by the hand and said, "Let's run!" Coming out at the end of that tunnel, I was laughing. I knew we'd make it to Grandmother's house. We did, sometime around mid-morning. Believe me, there was consternation in the family that day. My grandmother was furious; my mother showed up not much later, explaining that they'd had a broken axle coming back from a picnic on the Warrior River. The end of that little adventure was that come September my sister and I were safely stashed in Blessed Sacrament Academy, a Roman Catholic convent, where my mother was sure we'd have better supervision.

True, of course, but my traveling days were limited for a while.

Walking was the only way I could get anywhere besides riding a streetcar. Sunday afternoons I would cajole friends to walk a mile and a half to Elmwood Cemetery, where we'd picnic at the Dovel family plot. The picnic would be crackers with peanut butter. The Alabama Education Association's spring holidays gave me a chance to organize hikes to Red Mountain, where we would investigate old mine shafts. Before I was sixteen, with no driver's license, I was driving my mother's first automobile—it was 1945? yeah, 1945. The war was almost over, and Mother bought a used Army Ford V-8, painted flat black for the black-outs that were required on the East Coast during the war. My recollection is she paid $150 for it, and learning to drive a stick shift on the hills of Birmingham was a trick. But honey, it didn't bother me. I learned to keep my foot on the brake at the same time my heel was on the accelerator to keep that car from going backwards on the hills when I had to stop. My mother actually let me drive that car to club meetings and other high school events, and it went lots of places around Birmingham on Saturday nights.

Chapter Fourteen

Get A Relaxed Attitude
Traveling with Children

Road tripping by yourself is considerably different from road tripping with seven children. One thing I found out emphatically was that their daddy wasn't the least bit interested in going more than three miles in a car with seven children. When I mentioned camping as an option, he said, "Camping? I did all the camping I ever intend to do in the South Pacific in World War II." So I planned my first major camping trip with the children for a spring break.

Brice and Pickering by then were adept Boy Scouts. Fitzmaurice was a Cub Scout, and the rest of us didn't have the faintest idea of what to do in a campground. Nor did we have the right equipment. Undaunted, each week all winter I bought a couple of cans of food for the camp trip—Dinty Moore Stew, pork and beans, dry milk, packets of breakfast cereal—hoarding up boxes of food to put in the back of the VW bus. Come the end of March, we set out. We headed for the West Virginia Mountains—and it gets really cold in West Virginia the end of March. We were sleeping in old Army blankets I had stitched together to make sleeping bags, and we curled up against each other in the VW bus at night. (One morning we woke up and found the windshield covered with ice.) The thing I liked most about the camping was I didn't have to do anything. When we got to a campsite, I'd take my folding chair out and put it under a tree and tell those talented Boy Scouts to make a fire and heat up those cans of food. Those children were so darling. The best thing I learned on those cold mornings in those quiet camp grounds was to drive to the nearest small town, find a laundromat that was open, use their facilities, wash a load of clothes, clean up the children, and let them sit on top of the washing machine while they ate dry corn flakes and oranges. They were always so happy to see the laundry carts. The little children entertained each other by pushing them around like they were wagons. Baby Martha had her second birthday on our first camping trip. She was an inveterate traveler from then on.

My cousin Eloise and her husband, Bert Arnold, live in Houston, Texas, and, I know this is hard to believe, they have 13 children. It's a yours, mine, and ours family. She had four when her first husband died, Bert had four when his wife died, they married and proceeded to have five. My mother was then working in Houston. One March vacation I decided to go visit my cousin with my seven children. The major purpose of the trip was to see the whooping cranes, a dying species, which wintered in Port Arkansas

Wildlife Refuge. (We had discovered the whooping crane refuge from a long article in the National Geographic. The Boy Scouts were anxious to see a whooping crane.)

My cousin Eloise lived in a suburban house in Pasadena, Texas, with an enormous addition built to accommodate those 13 children. There was a big room on the second floor for the boys and a big dormitory room for the girls. The cleverest thing I ever saw in that house designed for 13 children was a hairbrush on a long chain, screwed to the wall in the bathroom. Eloise's husband is an engineer.

Anyhow, it was spring break for them, too, and we had 20 children darting in and out of the house. My mother came over for breakfast one morning and Eloise and I were serving pancakes. Do you have any idea how long it takes to make pancakes for 20 children? We cooked and cooked on Eloise's over-sized gas range for surely more than an hour. As the numbers were gradually diminishing around the long, long kitchen table, I sat down for a cup of coffee. My black-eyed child, John, was sitting at the table, the only one left, tears rolling down his cheeks. He looked at me with those big eyes and said, "Mama, didn't nobody never feed me." Sometimes children got lost in the shuffle. We made him a big stack of pancakes.

I also had a friend in Houston from my college days, Ann Waldron. Her husband, Martin, was an investigative reporter for the New York Times, on assignment in New Orleans. She had four children. Ann and I were having tea one afternoon, and I was telling her about our planned trip to see the whooping cranes. Her second child, Peter, said, "Mama, can't I go with them? I almost never get to see the Shearburns." At that, her third child Tommy said, "Fitz is my friend, and I want to go too so I can play with him." Lolly, the oldest child, said, "Well, if they're going to get to go then I ought to go too." Boogie, Ann's six-year-old, stood at the door sniffling, "I never get to go anywhere." And Ann, with her feet propped up on a hassock leaning back contentedly in a chair, said airily, "Oh, it's okay. All of you can go. And Dudley, as long as you're taking all the children, take Ju-Ju"—that was her black French poodle. And then she grinned and said, "While you are looking at whooping cranes, I'm going to fly to New Orleans and spend a couple of days with Martin." And she did.

Mercy, what a trip. Eleven children and the yapping dog in a VW bus, stacked on top with camping equipment. But it was absolutely glorious weather, a splendid spring on the Texas Gulf coast. Just the weather for travel.

When I drove into Goose Island State Park, I stopped at the forest ranger's office to inquire about a suitable campsite. He looked at that VW full of jumping children and said, "Ma'

101

am, follow me. I'll show you the best camp site in the park." I followed him, and we drove quite a way, slowly winding through the mesquite trees. When he stopped and pointed to a spot, I understood why he'd been so courteous. He had taken us a good 3/4 mile from any other campers. I suppose he thought isolation would serve us best.

I need to tell you we never saw one whooping crane. When I went to the wildlife refuge and walked in the office with those eleven children, the park ranger said, "Ma'am, did you make a reservation for your youth group?" Of course, I had not. But they made allowances anyhow and lent us binoculars and pointed us to a little road. There were blinds built up in the trees with a ladder leading to a small spot where you were to sit quietly, focus the binoculars, and look for the arrival of the birds. As it turned out, Martha, age three, was terrified of ladders and heights. She screamed the whole time we were in one of those blinds. That seemed effectively to scare off the whooping cranes.

The Shearburns have another favorite travel story. Let me tell you about Colonel Rogers. I was reading the personals in the At-lantic in April of '71. I saw his ad: Hunter's Cabin, Laramie Mt. Range. $250 for 6 weeks. Running water. (I later discovered that was not absolutely true. There was a faucet a half block away and an outhouse.) Of course it was too good to pass up. I rented the cabin sight unseen, and come summer, we were off. All seven children were still at home, and we didn't have any money. I had bought the cheapest car I could find for $1800 new, a two-door white Gremlin. Room enough for four people at most. It was the first summer I had taught on a 12-month salary, and I had a good half-summer off. In the Gremlin were Pickering and his girl friend, Geneva; Fitzmaurice, and I. Brice went out earlier on the Greyhound bus, and the Colonel picked him up in Cheyenne.

We had all the Boy Scout camping equipment, bedding, a WWII wooden sea-chest tied to the top of the car, a Gibson five-string banjo, a guitar, and hiking staffs and boots and hats, canvas backpacks from the Army & Navy Surplus Store, and foxhole shovels. We had a small tent and two WWII jungle hammocks (the hammocks were to hang up in trees to sleep in so the bears wouldn't bother us). We were ready for Wyoming, we thought. But there was no way we could have been ready for the Circle R Ranch, owner Colonel William Rogers, U.S. Army Retired.

It was hot. It was really hot in the Mid-West the middle of July, and this Gremlin hadn't even heard of air conditioning. We drove across Nebraska with plastic bags filled with ice on top of our heads. We were singing camp songs. When we got to Cheyenne, I thought something was wrong with the Gremlin because it was using too much gas. We stopped at a gas station, and the mechanic patiently explained that altitude made a difference in gas consumption. And that's when I realized we were going to the Rocky Mountains. But I still didn't know what was in store for us.

We drove 100 miles dead straight north from Cheyenne to Wheatland, Wyoming, and then we took a 90-degree turn to the west. I'd never seen such straight roads in my whole life. There are rancher, park service, and firefighter roads—not what we think of as "roads" exactly. As we made our way up toward the Laramie Mountain peaks, I began to notice that every car we saw—and there weren't too many—was 4-wheel drive. That tired little Gremlin, loaded down as it was, was struggling up. Of course we got lost in the mountains on narrow dirt roads, canyons on both sides. At one point the Gremlin couldn't make the grade, and I had to roll back about a block, get a running start, gun the engine, and head for the hills. We finally found the Circle R and Colonel Rogers. He was standing by a fence post having waited two hours, a tall white-headed man waving a big brimmed hat, sort of WWI field-variety, and dressed in combat fatigues and heavy army boots. As we pulled up, he pointed to his Ford Bronco and yelled, "Follow me!" and jumped into his car and took off.

For six weeks we lived in a cabin with no

running water. We cooked outside under a circle of pines, we took mountain walks, we met fascinating old Wyoming pioneers, ate cinnamon rolls with our neighbor three miles away—she made them and invited us over. Mail came twice a week on Tuesdays and Fridays. Sometime to have something to do we'd walk a mile and a half to the mailbox.

One of the most interesting developments of the summer was the Colonel's relationship with the children. Here we had three longhaired hippies, great devotees of the counter-culture, and probably in Colonel Rogers we had one of the most reactionary conservatives in Wyoming. (Wyoming is a state filled with reactionary conservatives.) But the Colonel hired the three little hippies to work on his road. He would knock on the door to our cabin at seven in the morning, announce himself, "Colonel Rogers here. Miss Geneva, Pickering, Fitzmaurice, time to get up. Coffee in ten minutes. Pickering, tell your mother the coffee will be ready in ten minutes." Of course I was standing right there; I could hear him. But Colonel Rogers was accustomed to a chain of command.

He had those teenagers digging, smoothing, carrying gravel in their shirts, and he promised to pay them at the end of the holiday. And he did, true to his word. The three of them griped a little bit, laughed a lot, and to this day love to talk about Colonel Rogers and his road building. They did a great job.

If we heard a car twice a week, we got really excited. We'd sit on the cabin stoop when we heard a car in the distance and say, "Listen, listen, I think somebody's coming!" The road was seldom used, but Colonel Rogers daily reminded us to keep the Gremlin out of the turn-around: we must keep the turn-around clear. It was as though we might suddenly have to make some hurried escape from the circle of old Wyoming cabins that seldom attracted visitors. The other guests included two women from New York who were going to write a book: they stayed a week, they couldn't stand it, it was too remote. The Colonel's lady friend, Virginia Sculley, lived in the best house in what the Colonel referred to as "the compound." Virginia Sculley was a writer who at one time was recognized as an authority on Indian herb medicine. However, she was a little dotty and in a state of decline the summer we shared with her in Wyoming.

Colonel Rogers taught us a lot: we cooked antelope over an open fire, we learned about the terrible massacre of the Cheyennes, we swam (and took our baths) in the reservoir twenty miles away. We carried water for the dishes from a faucet 300 yards down the hill. Pick and Geneva and Fitzmaurice dammed up a mountain stream to make a bathing pool, but the water was too icy to put your foot in. Brice didn't stay— he left with the New York writers. He began a friendship with the young women who were in their twenties, and they drove away. He had his long hair tied back, he was as brown and as handsome as an Indian, and he waved goodbye out the window.

The third week, Martha flew out from St. Louis. She was six years old and flew by herself to Denver. But she was afraid to sleep in the cabin because chipmunks ran around the ceiling at night. So Martha and I slept in a pup tent under the pines, our heads sticking out, looking at the stars. I'd tell her stories until she went to sleep. Up this god-forsaken, remote, treacherous road drove four different carloads of people from St. Louis. I had told everybody I was going to have a party, and they were invited. Seemed like they all came, and the arrivals of cars with friends from St. Louis were major events. My friend Nancy Mathews, who had taught with me in the St. Louis ghetto, came in a huge old Oldsmobile with her mother and her two nieces. They were on their way back home, having driven to Alaska, and they arrived with four tires tied to the top of the car. Nancy had thought she'd bought the best tires in St. Louis, guaranteed to withstand the Al-Can highway. Before they ever got to Fairbanks, the tires were completely worn out. Determined, she tied them on the top of the car to return them to the dealer and get her money back.

On Mondays we went to Wheatland for supplies. One Monday as I was walking down the

107

street in Wheatland, near-sighted as I am, I looked across the street and I said, "Pickering, that guy looks like Tom Morgan." Turned out it was Tom Morgan from St. Louis. He took us up on our invitation and stayed three weeks, but he didn't work on the Colonel's road. Tom was a history teacher and he came to read and rest. He told the Colonel he was "down in the back."

The crowning experience was a three-day trip planned by Colonel Rogers. This involved three automobiles. The Colonel, Pick, Geneva, and Fitz left in the Colonel's Ford Bronco. Martha and I left a day later in the Gremlin, and Tom drove his old Ford Fairlane because he wanted to make a side trip to the Black Hills of South Dakota. It would be hard to imagine any troop movement involving any more maps and planning than this trip to northern Wyoming, South Dakota, and Nebraska. The Colonel had maps and compasses and a notebook and kept saying, "This is Checkpoint Charlie, here by the anthropological dig in Northwest Wyoming." This was how he'd planned the trip when we'd sat out under the pines. "This is Checkpoint Charlie, Mrs. Shearburn." He gave me explicit instructions as to U.S. highways, state roads, county roads, to get to a site he wanted us to see. I was admonished to arrive at Checkpoint Charlie, marked on my map with a big red X at 1400 the day after his departure. Martha and I left the mountain the day after the children and the

Colonel had departed, followed his instructions, left at the exact time he told us to leave, and, would you believe it, we came down that county road at 1400 and saw Pick jump up from a ditch waving his hat. They met us at the appointed spot and took us to the dig. We camped one night with a full moon by a reservoir in North Dakota, made a one-day trip to Deadwood for Pioneer Day, ate buffalo burgers in South Dakota, and spent a wonderful, instructive day at Ft. Robinson in Western Nebraska. One thing about Colonel Rogers: he was bound and determined we were going to learn something, and learn a lot we did.

By the end of our visit the Colonel was a solid friend of the three teenagers. Fitzmaurice was his favorite, and when we left he gave Fitz a Mexican blanket and a pair of leather chaps that had belonged to a turn-of-the-century cowboy. To this very day forty-year-old Fitzmaurice prizes those gifts from his trip west. And to this very day I stay in close touch with Colonel Rogers, now 90, bright of mind, living in a retirement center in Scribner, Nebraska. Recently I said in a phone call, "Bill, how are you?" and he shot back, irritably, "How do you think I am—I am 90 years old with arthritis." But he's tough, and he's determined. He always says to me, as he did the other day when I called, what wonderful children I have, how glad he is they're doing well. When the children talk about Colonel Rogers, they talk about what a taskmaster he was.

He calls me Dudley now. And I call him Bill. Martha had him to dinner in California two years ago. Holley and I drove to Scribner, west of Omaha, Nebraska, to see him this past summer. He really is a kind of fixture in the family.

In the fall of 1979 during fall break at Salem College, I signed on for a four-day cheap-budget trip to the Yucatan. Our destination was Mérida capital of this distant rural province; but of course while I was there, I looked around and found a place for the Shearburns in the small port town of Progresso, twenty-five miles to the north. I could remember about twenty words of high school Spanish, which I tried out on a Mérida realtor (Se renta? Como cuesta? Quando es posible? Por la Navidad?). After lots of smiles and a $100 deposit, I signed a lease for a month— from December 21 to January 21. The house was huge, right on the Gulf, with five bedrooms, a gorgeous terrace, louvered shutters for the breezes to come in. The only furniture was a big table in the dining room and about a dozen scattered straight chairs in various rooms. There was a charcoal brazier stove, which looked like a barbecue pit. There were a couple of worn-out pans and a refrigerator that wasn't plugged in. As the realtor showed me around, I made mental notes: someone would have to fix the frayed cord on the refrigerator. It was only when I was flying home that I thought to wonder where we would all sleep.

I came back to tell the children about the perfect house—its name, San Pedro, was carved over the door—with sun shining on the cream stone and a view of the Gulf and the feel of breezes in the palms and banana trees. And so as promised, on December 21 I flew (with daughter Martha) as the advance guard to prepare for the various arrivals of the Shearburns and our friends. I had worked out the cheapest of all cheap airfares. We'd drive the car from North Carolina to New Orleans, park it in a friend's backyard, and take Aviateca Airlines, a Guatemalan airlines, to Mérida for $109 round trip. The other children from St. Louis—is that where everybody was?—traveled the same way, driving from St. Louis to New Orleans.

Aviateca Airlines is a story all by itself. The departure schedule was somewhat willy-nilly. My recollection is that the plane was three hours late leaving, and the pilot and co-pilot served as desk clerk, baggage clerk, and pilots. But $109, you couldn't beat that anywhere. So for about $2,000, I had arranged a one-month vacation for the eight Shearburns. I invited every friend I knew to come down and share our mansion by the sea, and the startling thing was most of them came.

My remembrance of that month is mostly meeting airplanes, finding bed rolls for people to sleep on, and trying to get meals together for up to 16 people. (Christmas Day is a blur, as it always is wherever you are.) We plugged in the refrigerator, which immediately showed itself to be an enemy. Every time you touched the metal handle, you got a mild shock. Fitzmaurice, the Mr. Fix-it of our family, taped a block of wood to the handle, and he became forever the best friend of our Maya cook, Chela.

When our dear friend, Colonel Rogers, came from Wyoming, other needs were taken care of with his usual commanding presence. The Colonel went to the town square and hired Chela for $10 a week plus room and board. Now you think that sounds really cheap? But here's what you got when you got Chela. You got her 13-month-old baby, Jessica, and her 16-year-old cousin, Lis, who came to baby-sit the baby. They, of course, joined us at table for every meal. Chela was only 18 herself, and one of the things I found out was that Chela and Lis were afraid to stay at the house by themselves at night. "Ladrones!" Chela would say: robbers, they might come. (They didn't.) So when the family and I and assorted visitors went into Mérida for a night out, I had to hire a baby-sitter to keep Chela, Jessica, and Lis. Not to mention the fact that Chela got the best room in the house, the one on the second floor that faced the Gulf—cool and quiet so the baby's nap wouldn't be interrupted.

The next best room went to Colonel Rogers. It had a private bath and, after all, he was the ranking officer. You want to know where we slept in that house with no furniture? The realtor assured me that it was a simple matter of hammocks. String hammocks, they could be bought on any corner of any street in Mérida for a nominal price. We loaded up with hammocks the day we went out to Progresso. After one night it was obvious to me that sleeping in hammocks was going to take some practice. You have to learn to sleep on the diagonal.

I've got to tell you this story about how we solved the problem. Colonel Rogers said he knew a place that sold foam rubber by the yard. Colonel Rogers believes in budgets and thrift. We rode the local bus into the city. The Colonel, retired from the engineer corps of World War II, had on campaign boots and a Smoky Bear hat. I trailed behind. We bought four huge rolls of foam rubber tied with string, two for him and two for me to carry back to the house on the local bus with the chickens, the babies, the Mexican mothers, and the singing bus driver. Religious pendants swung from the mirror and must have blessed us all the way. When we got home, we turned those rubber mats into comfortable beds, and everyone sighed. I could hear them all over the house.

Tips for traveling

Don't try to please everybody.

Plan the vacation and let the kids adjust.

Try to find out-of-the-way places.

Be sure to take along some children. They see the world through different eyes

Try to keep a budget in mind.

Pay for things ahead of time.

Avoid unexpected expenses.

Stay away from hotels Americans frequent.

No trip is perfect. Expect the unexpected and do the best you can at the moment.

Look at the big picture and keep in mind this is for fun not stress.

Look for the easiest way out of a problem.

It's great fun to be in markets and buy the artifacts of the region. Just know when you get home you'll wonder why you bought them.

Chapter Fifteen

🌢

Get A Ticket
Seeing the World

Now let's talk about the walking trip in Ireland two years ago. The way these trips get born is I have to go somewhere. I have to fill up any spare time I have. I have to think about where I'm going to go. I had read in *Ireland of the Welcomes* about walking trips in Ireland, and I had read in *Travel and Leisure* that the Russian airlines—Aeroflot—is the cheapest, shortest way to get to Ireland. The tour offered a week for about $900 for everything. Pick you up at Shannon airport, take you to Western Ireland, a week in a B&B, three meals a day, van service to wherever you were going to start your walk. One of the real pluses was that the little village—Sneem—was going to have a one-week Irish homecoming the week we were there. All the children would be coming home to see their mothers and daddies, and that meant there was going to be a party every night.

Did I say that at the time there were stories in the news about poor performance airlines—like Aeroflot—which had been de-nationalized or whatever they did to Russian industry with the collapse of the Soviet Union?

So now these two things are put together—a cheap airline and a cheap walking trip. Does it worry me that the airline isn't safe? My sons all informed me how foolish I was to be flying Aeroflot. But that's all right. I wanted the experience. I wanted to fly out of Washington, the fastest trip to Europe, and I thought it would be fun.

The summer of the collapse of the Soviet Union, every other American was taking a trip to Russia. Delta manages the Aeroflot desk at Dulles; so there was somebody who speaks English. I received my ticket, and about a week before departure this woman at Delta called and said, "I can give you a seat assignment, but it won't make any difference because nobody sits in an assigned seat." That was my first clue about what this airline was going to be like. My son in Washington dropped me off at Dulles, and I loved it. This was going to be a snap. And then I walked into the terminal and I saw these people—119 Americans lining up for a tour to Russia, and then there was me. And sure enough, I was the only one with a seat assignment. They took us out to the plane on one of those shuttle things, and here's this wonderful big safe-looking Soviet plane out there with English-speaking Delta agents taking tickets. And then everybody got on the plane. People were just pushing down the aisles, sitting anywhere they wanted to sit, but I had a seat assignment, and I looked up to find my seat row 13, seat or whatever. I was puzzled because I kept looking at the numbers and you couldn't tell which row they indicated. As I was looking around, a man said, "Don't worry, just sit down. They put in extra rows." So the seating was close, and row numbers didn't matter. I took a seat that had nothing to do with my assignment, and an elderly American couple sat down next to me and we agreed that it was a good thing we were not very big people because our knees were up to our chins. People were sitting down wherever they wanted to sit and putting things in the overhead bins.

My seat belt didn't work, so I tapped the flight attendant and said, "My seat belt doesn't work." She shrugged her shoulders and said, "Okay," which I found out was the only English she knew. As we got ready to take off, there were bins that didn't close, so I pointed them out to the attendant and said, "The bins didn't close." She smiled and said, "Okay," and so we took off with several overhead bins open and I don't know how many seat belts not working. It's about 5 hours 45 minutes from Dulles to Shannon. I pulled out the safety instructions and read about the plane, and I knew it was a good plane, and Delta did their maintenance in Washington, so I didn't have any sense of not being safe. The flight attendants smoked, walking up and down the aisles. The vodka was free, and people were drinking and talking and moving around. Men were standing around in the back, smoking cigarettes and drinking vodka. It was a little different. It was casual. They served three meals and we laughed because you couldn't determine which meal was served for what. Was this breakfast served at suppertime, or was it a snack? There were lots of beets, beet soup, sliced beets. When we arrived at Shannon, there were only four of us getting off, and the rest were going to Moscow. It was three o'clock in the morning when we arrived, and guess what?—they couldn't find our luggage. So they must have unloaded by hand a good bit of the cargo bay, and about an hour later they had found our luggage. So I was in Ireland on a cheap flight, and it was worth every penny of it.

I had been on walking trips in England over the years, and walking trips in England were much more expensive than this one. The walking trips in England were very elegant, very lively. The guides meet you at a designated place with two station wagons, and they take you to a stately home where you are going to stay all week. You meet for breakfast, and you walk a couple of hours, and then you stop for coffee at a country pub and walk a couple more hours, and the station wagons bring a tail-gate lunch, with a good wine, and then you sit and chat and then you walk a little while longer, and then you stop for tea, and then you go back to the stately home, and go into the library and have a drink, and go upstairs and take a bath and a nap, and then you dress for dinner, about 8:30 or 9. We had servers, nice young women in black uniforms with white aprons. It was all very nice. We walked about eight miles a day. I could do that, so I thought that was what it was going to be like in Ireland.

But that wasn't the way it was in Ireland. The young man who owned the Irish walking company—Jim McDonald—looked as though he had been teaching in Outward Bound. He had on those short shorts like they wear in the Alps and knee length socks and heavy boots. He looked more like a mountain climber than my British walking leader, who looked British. (On my British walking tour they assured you that it was not going to be too strenuous, and if you wanted only a half-day you could go back to the stately home.) But now we had Jim McDonald in Western Ireland. He wasn't very talkative in the van from Shannon. We picked up people at Shannon and Kenmare, and there were some people who had gotten there early to the village of Sneem. Fourteen people on this walking trip.

It was called a moderate walk. It was not supposed to be demanding or challenging. But I began to realize as the group gathered that we had some serious walkers. Some of them had spent the week before walking in the Wicklow Mountains with Jim McDonald. A couple of them were Dutch, and there was one from Belgium, and there was an English couple, get this, on their honeymoon. Brian and Annie. And then there were a couple of English schoolteachers who take a walking trip every summer. My first real clue that I was among professional walkers was when Jim McDonald said, "Did everybody bring gaiters?" Do you know what gaiters are? They are like puttees in WWI that go over the trousers legs to protect them from rain and mud. He said, "It's likely to rain tomorrow. It may rain every day you're here. So it's likely to be a trifle muddy."

I looked at those people and said to myself, "These people know what they're doing. These walkers are serious." They had little maps and little map cases to keep the rain off their maps, and they had staffs, like walking canes, to help in case it got steep. They had binoculars and hats to protect themselves from the rain. And rain pants in addition to their gaiters, these goretex rain pants. I had my good goretex rainproof lace-up boots, and I had a sleeveless vest with pockets, but I didn't have binoculars or maps or map cases or any gaiters. And I didn't have any idea what Western Ireland was going to be like. I was thinking of green grass and rainbows and little roads and undulating hills and cottages tucked away here and there. Well, so much for that.

The next morning we gathered for breakfast, and Jim did our information session. We were going to walk across the fields and go up a couple of hills across a pasture and up some moderate hills and then we'd stop for lunch, we'd take a picnic. It would be easy, the afternoon would be an easy descent, and we'd get back about 4:30 or 5:00. Well, we got in a van and Jim McDonald drove us to our beginning place. We parked the van and started up a little road, and I thought, this is not too bad. I bet we hadn't walked a hundred yards before we were in a little lane that turned into big muddy ruts. Then Jim said cheerfully, "We're going to cut across this pasture," and then he pointed out the distant hill. And I'm telling you the god's truth, it was a mountain.

And it was raining; the pasture was like a bog. Every time I put my boot down, this sucking mud would come up to the top of my goretex walking boots. I'd pull my foot out, and there'd be this sucking sound. Then I'd put my foot in the next place, and my foot would sink down into black sucking mud. After about a half mile, I was exhausted. I had a horrible, horrible realization that this was going to go on for eight hours. I was going to have to go along. The salvation, of course, was the 14 wonderful people I met. It was raining, and there was not a trail, and so we were going up a rocky, barren hill, and I kept sliding on the wet rocks, and holding on to the rock ahead of me. They would wait for me to catch up, hold my hand, and pull me up when my legs started shaking. They said, "Sit down and rest, you're going to be okay." The English couple, school teachers, Gillian and Anthony, were just great. They would laugh at my hateful remarks like "I promise you God if I get down off this mountain I'll never go on another trip like this." And then there was Alexander. Alexander and Gillian and Anthony got me through that muddy slippery, rocky West Ireland hike.

It's hard to describe Alexander Kostka. He was the most even, kind-spoken, encouraging person that day. Alexander is a professor of modern German history at a university in the suburbs of Paris. Although he was born in Germany, he came to Paris when he was 15, and he's quick to tell you that he's French. He's a French citizen, and he lives in the City of Light, the most beautiful city in the world. Alexander is European, he's a gentleman, he appears to be formal; he really isn't. But on first meeting, he seems formal. I judged he was in his early or mid-thirties. Alexander looks exactly as a university academic should look: slender face, wire-rim glasses, a receding hairline, average height, not a bit corpulent. Each time I faltered, Alexander would inquire in his wonderful accented English, "Can I help you? Are you all right?" He would take my arm, shepherd me through a couple of steep mountain ways, going up, and in spite of my ill temper and exhaustion, he remained consistently cheerful. So that by the time we stopped for lunch, I was sure that this was one friend I was going to hold on to for life.

We finally stopped for lunch, on a soggy knoll—other people seemed to have had the foresight to bring plastic drop-cloths—and I sat myself down and in five minutes was wet on the rear end. Anyway, when we sat down for our picnic lunch, I had an opportunity to find out about the people who came for this week of walking. I spent time finding out about Alexander. He's a bachelor, who goes on several walking trips every summer, and he loves the U.S. He's a scholar who has been many places in the world, and he told me he hoped to be at the Getty Institute in California the following year. So, as I usually do, I said, "Oh, come visit N.C. and stay with me," which of course he did, the very next year.

About this walking trip: the next day I sent a message to Jim McDonald, the Alpine climber, and told him I was sick with a sore throat and thought I'd stay in bed. It was all a lie. There wasn't anything the matter with me except my legs were really sore, but that soft Irish rain told me I wasn't about to try another bog and another mountain. Instead, I spent that day investigating the town of Sneem. This village in Kerry had won the award the previous year as the tidiest town in Western Ireland. The village center was two blocks long with tiny shops, flowers at every door, a farm museum in an old shed with the collection lying about hit or miss, labeled on bits of paper in a kind of Spencerian script. The museum keeper was a museum piece himself. Of course, like most Irish villages, every other door was a pub, and I found out that because of the Sneem homecoming week, there would be amateur programs of music at various pubs each evening. I could hardly wait to tell Alexander.

The hikers came home from their second day of hiking looking strong, accomplished, and muddy. Their gaiters were spattered. I, on the other hand, had enjoyed a lovely lunch, a nice nap, a hot bath, had rolled up my hair, visited the museum, gone to the book store and bought books on Ireland, and could hardly wait to do the pubs.

Since I was taking a group of women to Paris in October, I was quick to tell Alexander we would look him up when we came. As the October trip materialized, I decided it would be good to include Alexander in some of the things we'd be doing. The trip was an outgrowth of the reading group called "Paris by Book and Foot" which met at the Rainbow Cafe in Winston-Salem. Eight women signed up to go on the trip. Of the eight, six of them I knew well because I had taught them in classes at Salem College. It was a trip designed for working women who want to travel but don't want to travel alone, and who can't be gone for a very long time—the trip was eight days. And it was a trip for people who love to read, of course. It was not going to be a tour, we weren't going to ride around on a bus, we'd stay in one place—in this instance, a wonderful French hotel on the Left Bank—the Lutetia. On this trip and other trips I've planned for women, the best rule is you get to sleep late. We don't do anything before 10:30 in the morning, and we go out every night. And somewhere in between, we try to see the famous tourist spots, but we reserve a lot of time for some offbeat special places. I promised this group that we'd walk and walk and walk—but not in mud.

The most famous avenue in the world is the Champs Elysses. The famous landmarks are the Arc de Triomphe, the Place de la Concorde, the Palais Royal, the Gamier Opera. The special places we'd discover for ourselves were Pere-Lachaise Cemetery, Parc Monceau, a picnic at the Medici fountain, a walk along the Seine on a misty evening, the Place Dauphin—a small park on the Ile de le Cite—the places where we really caught the spirit of Paris: the sophisticated metropolitan elegance of a city that is almost 1,000 years old, the enjoyment that Parisians obviously take in their small beautiful enclosed places, the ability to sit on a bench and just watch the world.

There's something both elegant and relaxed about the way Parisians enjoy their city, and it's in small unexpected places that you begin to feel as if you are a part of it.

Alexander may have provided the best

experience of Paris for all of us. Before we arrived, by long distance phone, he and I had agreed that he would have a wine and cheese buffet in his apartment near the Place Pigalle and that he would talk to my North Carolina friends about the history of Paris. He is a connoisseur of good wines, gives lots of thought to the matching of cheeses with certain wines. His apartment is a fifth-floor walk-up with windows from ceiling to floor, overlooking Montmartre. Nothing could be more characteristic of Paris. The apartment is a block and a half up a narrow side street from the Place Pigalle, and the Place Pigalle, of course, is the notorious racy, exotic sex shop center of what tourists consider erotic Paris, but Alexander's fifth floor apartment could not have been more removed. We had a code of numbers we pressed to gain entry; and from this busy Montmartre neighborhood, we went into the quiet, stone-floored foyer of a building built in the early 1800s. The steps were a lovely, worn, softly shining wood. The railings were elegantly wrought iron, the stair treads were covered with an Oriental runner and we followed it up. We entered Alexander's apartment through 14-foot, carved wooden doors and stepped into a foyer to be greeted by our host and led into his living room.

The apartment is as simple and plain as the building is ornate. The cove ceilings and plaster of Paris decorative moldings of the lovely old building are in contrast to his spare furnishings and modern art. He arranged us around his marble fireplace. Here were these women from North Carolina, and we were a long way from Winston-Salem, not just in terms of miles. Some had traveled before, some had not. At Alexander's we had wine and cheese and began to feel more comfortable. We talked about walking up six floors, the difference between the neighborhood on the street and the elegant privacy of a Paris apartment, the kind of life that urban Parisians lived. One of the things we wanted to see was the kitchen: small, utilitarian. It's not the way Americans live. We noticed that the sense of space comes from windows that look out, from a view, and maybe that's why Parisians use their parks and sit on benches and walk by the Seine and stay outside and sit in cafes and are on the street until late at night. There's a vibrancy outside people's houses and inside Alex's apartment that makes you understand how people use their city and why Parisians use it as they do. The apartment overlooked the slope of Montmartre down to the Place Pigalle with its old apartment buildings, some with balconies, tall, slender buildings where people live with potted plants and awnings. We really got a sense of being in a very different place. Alexander made us feel his love for his city and his desire to share that appreciation and love.

At the end of our Paris trip when the other

women had returned home, I planned to go to Amsterdam for three or four days to see my son John and his wife Annette and their two children. They live in Amsterdam, where John is Consul General of the U.S. Consulate. I was especially eager to meet the new baby, Claire, and to bring her presents from North Carolina, especially the pretty dress I had bought at Carolina Thrift. So I wouldn't waste a minute of the lovely days in Paris and Amsterdam, I decided to take an overnight train.

In making these plans, I refused to think about how I hated foreign train stations. Electronic boards announcing departures and arrivals in foreign languages, the whole notion of trains leaving on split-second schedules, leaving no time for mistakes, give me the shivers, but I wanted an extra day in Paris; so it was the night train.

Alexander, knowing how I hate the confusion of the huge train station, Gare du Nord, agreed to come to my hotel, go with me in a taxi, and put me on the 11:30 p.m. train. There was a small problem with the night train, but I whisked right over that. Things would work out fine. There's no first-class sleeping car service midweek from Paris to Amsterdam, so the only choice is second-class, couchette. It sounds sweet and relaxing, comfy, couch-like. It was only $27 extra; that should have tipped me off.

On Monday before my departure Wednesday evening, Alexander called, apologetic, saying he felt guilty knowing how I hate the train station by myself. However, circumstances involving his ladylove meant he would not be able to go with me to the train station on Wednesday. Alexander is dear and I didn't want him to feel bad. I assured him I would manage fine. Then I had a great idea: I suggested to Alexander that we do a run-through on Tuesday night. He'd go with me, walk through the procedure, show me the track, and I'd feel better about going by myself on Wednesday. Alexander loved the solution and he said, "There's a wonderful restaurant across from the station. We'll have a leisurely dinner and go over to the station at 11:00, and I'll show you exactly where to get the train."

And so he picked me up for dinner at 8:30. The restaurant was splendid, and the food was wonderful. My recollection is we drank a bottle and a half of good wine. We walked over to the train station, happy and laughing, I was sure it was going to work out fine. There were a few intricacies it was good to know about. One, I never would have figured out the post at the head of each track, where there's a little notch in the post and it's very important to slip the ticket in and get an automatic stamp. Nobody tells you about that unless you have a friend like Alexander. If you don't have your ticket stamped and you get on the train, there's a fine. So I felt good about our practice run.

Alexander showed me the board where the train would be announced, pointed out to me that I had to get on the right sleeper since one of the cars switches off and heads for Germany in the middle of the night. That was good to know. He showed me how to find the number of my car and pointed out it was a long, long train, so I should be sure my luggage was well organized since I would have to walk about 20 cars down the platform to get to my car.

Wednesday night, I got there early, worried about foolish things like maybe the train wouldn't come or would be on a different track. The French being French, the train was posted at exactly the same time as the preceding night on exactly the same track, posted to leave at exactly 11:32 p.m. All was going well. As Alexander had instructed me, I walked past a long string of train cars, found the right number of the sleeping car, and noticed a big jam of people pushing to get up the steps and into the car. There are a couple of things about a couchette I didn't know. First of all, there is an extremely narrow aisle that leads to the cubicles where you sleep. Negotiating luggage took some skill. But here's what I didn't know. These are the sleeping arrangements: there are eight cubicles in the car. Each little cubicle has a narrow opening that leads to a narrow aisle and on each side of the aisle in the cubicle are three bunks. That means there are six sleeping places in each cubicle. It is a second-class sleeper. There are a folded blanket, a folded sheet, and a pillow on each bunk. You sleep in your clothes, it seems, and your sleeping mates are the luck of the draw. On this particular night going from Paris to Amsterdam, almost the entire car was filled with Chinese from Taiwan, puffing cigarettes, talking excitedly, trying to understand the signs posted along the passageway. I was doing the same thing, and I can't read French. I did notice their consternation at the posted "No Smoking" signs. They kept pointing, shaking their heads, puffing their cigarettes, until the conductor came through before the train departed and reminded them not to smoke.

I had stepped into my cubicle with four young Chinese gentlemen. Clearly, they were my overnight mates to Amsterdam. On the top bunk, a young Frenchman leaned over and said in perfect English, "Good evening, can I help you with your luggage? You're on the third bunk. But that's the best bunk, you have more room."

It turned out his name was Jules; his mother was French, his father was Dutch. He was twenty years old, taking a break from college, and had been a waiter in the French Alps during the ski season. We laughed a little and gradually settled down with our books. Jules had put my luggage at the foot of my bunk. It seems that with the pillow, the blanket, and the sheet, you also sleep with your suitcase. He explained to me that the overhead lights would automatically go out and we would have a reading light, and he showed me where to turn it off. I propped up to read, and the four Chinese gentlemen settled down to sleep.

After about ten minutes, Jules said, "It's hot in here!" and pushed the window down. We both felt that cool breeze and settled back to read. Our traveling companion in bunk number 2 got up and closed the window. Jules looked at me and smiled. "Hmmm, well, wait until he goes to sleep." We read for another 20 minutes until Jules said, "You think he's asleep?" and I said, "I believe he is." Our top bunks were a little warmish. Jules stretched over and pushed the window down again. The sleeping Chinese got up and closed it.

It looked as if a warm night on the couchette was ahead, and we settled down to sleep. I had taken two Excedrins and two Ibuprofens and I was determined to sleep. Then just as I was drifting off to sleep, I heard from one of the Chinese sleepers a deep resonant loud snore. "Oh, no," I said. "Jules, this is like being married."

The snorer turned over, wiggled, and his friend under him reached up, gave him a punch, hoping too he'd settle down. The snorer stopped snoring, the Excedrin took effect, Jules turned out his reading light, and my experience on the second-class couchette turned out to be not so bad after all.

I woke up as we pulled into The Hague at daylight, was fifth in line for the ladies' bathroom, and managed to look presentable by the time we came into the station at Amsterdam. It was good to see John and Annette with the babies at the station. Now I know about couchettes. Not bad at all for $27.00. Besides, I'd met Jules.

There are other trips I could tell about. When Alexander came to visit me in my apartment in Winston-Salem, I took him to my house trailer in Sparta in the mountains of North Carolina, and we took a Sunday brunch boat cruise on the New River. Then there was the ferry ride from Rafina, Greece, to northern Kavala. A week in a Greek village where I had pomegranate juice from fruit picked that morning. When in Chichester, England, in a B&B run by John and Paul, we drove to the medieval seaport of Bosham. In Taos, New Mexico, in a rented adobe house where the children came to ski in January. There I saw the erotic paintings of D.H. Lawrence tucked away in the office of an old hotel. Tallahassee, Florida, and I took my seven children to visit my old friends Ann and Martin Waldron, and we celebrated Martin's Pulitzer Prize with a shrimp boil. En route to the San Antonio Hemisfair in 1968, the seven children and I traveling in our VW bus spent a night by a lake near Texarkana, swatting mosquitoes. But these stories are for another time.

My children are all grown, and they don't

133

travel with me anymore. But I'm growing me a new companion. She's Holley, the daughter of Mary. She turned eight during our one-month train trip from Winston-Salem to Washington, Chicago, San Francisco, El Paso, Ft. Worth, St. Louis, back through Chicago, Washington, and home.

First-class deluxe. We had booked a sleeping compartment on Amtrak. The longest leg from Chicago to San Francisco was super deluxe, living room and bedroom. The most delightful thing to Holley and me was a hot shower every day. Porter service included a chocolate on your pillow when he prepared your berth at night. Great dining car food was made better because each meal you shared your table with another traveler. We met a wonderful John from Glasgow, an interesting John from Chicago, and a couple from Ft. Worth on the way to Michigan for their 52nd wedding anniversary. Holley said, "You've been married 52 years? Why, dear you don't look a day over 52 yourself!" When they got off the train, the lady told me they'd never met a smarter eight-year-old.

Holley read and played games, and every night her night-light was on when I on the bottom bunk drifted off to sleep. We arrived in Denver at 7 a.m. and crossed the Rocky Mountains and went through a snowstorm at Lake Tahoe. Holley had an aim-and-shoot camera. Her snapshot of an El Paso sunset looks like a Rothko painting. The

Amtrak cars are double-deck observations all the way, including the sleepers, the dining car, and the lounge car. We had a perfect view of the American landscape. The train came into San Francisco across the bay at Emeryville, just at dark. We looked across the bay at the Christmas lights of San Francisco. Holley wrote in her journal, "There was a window shield factory of minus 45 and the soles of my shoes froze in Chicago, where we spent three days."

Chapter Sixteen

Get it Together
Youth & Age

Friends have often said to me, "You need to write a book, why don't you write a book?" And my friend Emily made my life easier by helping me write it. I think what they were saying is that my life experiences have been a little off the mark, a little eccentric, a little outside the rule, just a little—that's what they laugh about. They ask: "How'd you do that? How could you? God, I wouldn't be able to do that. What were you thinking of?" I say, "Write your own script, do it like you want to do it, live your own life, don't let people tell you what to do." And that's what my friends are interested in about me, I think. Live it up, don't live it down. When I went to therapy years ago, I used to say to my therapist, Elizabeth Garlington, "I have a rage to live. I've got to." I want to pass along my rage to live.

I think I have passed it along in my own family. Recently, my sons John and Brice and my granddaughter Holley were having dinner at the Zevely House in Winston-Salem, our favorite restaurant. I was to join them later because I was teaching late at Salem College. The boys and Holley were seated at a table in an upstairs dining room. (They always put us in a private room, I think, because we make so much noise. I used to think it was because we were special customers.) Before dinner came, the boys went downstairs to visit friends at the bar while Holley was moving around the restaurant greeting her own friends. (Holley goes a couple of times a week with Brice while her mother, Mary, works at night at the hospital.) When John and Brice returned to the table, Holley wasn't there, so they decided to take advantage of her absence to conduct a little family business. They wanted to talk about Mom's living arrangements. John insisted that the downtown neighborhood where I had chosen to live was unsafe, and furthermore, the apartment was too small. He tried to convince Brice it was time for me to move to the suburbs to a nicer neighborhood and a nicer place. John had pad and pen in hand to show Brice how it was financially feasible for me to move. Brice listened, Brice agreed. They had it all worked out: Mom would move.

At that moment, Holley, who had hidden herself under the table, pushed aside the cloth and jumped out, and shouted, hands on hip, "You can't do that! Grandma loves her apartment! Grandma can do what she wants to do! She's the boss!"

And that ended the discussion of moving me out.

I heard about this scene when I arrived.

Brice was laughing, Holley hugged me and said, "I told 'em," and John put away his pen and pad.

The Shearburn women run their own lives. I learned to stand up for myself from my mother and grandmother; and Holley learned it from her mother and me. The tradition lives on.

Dudley Shearburn is a reader, teacher, traveler and free spirit. She entertains her seven grown children (and seven grandchildren,) hundreds of students, and countless friends with stories that only Dudley could tell—hilarious, adventuresome and wise. Her travel groups and book discussions in Winston-Salem, North Carolina, have made her a local celebrity. With the publication of *Get a Good Life*, her fame reaches from Tallapoosa, Alabama to Paris, France. Now a professor emeritus of Salem College, she is free to wander at will.

Emily Wilson is a teacher and writer whose books of poetry and women's history are tame in comparison to her books with Dudley. These are written while coffee brews, the phone rings and laughter erupts. Emily teaches Dudley how to get her words into print, Dudley teaches Emily how to find treasures in junk shops, cheap gifts for priceless friends and relaxed party atmospheres. Together they talk about their precious children, their occasional mistakes and their good lives.

WildWood Press was founded in 1996 by Emily and her sister, Janis Herring Eberhardt, who lives, teaches and edits manuscripts in their hometown of Columbus, Georgia.

1-336-721-1957   27,08
P.O.Box 10277 W-S NC

For additonal copies of
Get a Good Life,
mail this form with your check or money order to:

WildWood Press
2616 Village Trail
Winston-Salem, NC 27106-2332

Name: _____

Address: _____

_____

City/State/Zip:_____

Telephone: _____

Quantity _____ @ $9.99 $ _____

Add $3 shipping and handling. $ _____
Add $2 each additional copies mailed.

NC residents add a 6% sales tax $ _____
of $.60 for each copy ordered.

TOTAL $ _____